ROSAMOND LEHMANN
AN APPRECIATION

Books by Rosamond Lehmann

Books by Gillian Tindall

ROSAMOND LEHMANN
An Appreciation

Gillian Tindall

CHATTO & WINDUS

THE HOGARTH PRESS

LONDON

Published in 1985 by
Chatto & Windus · The Hogarth Press
40 William IV Street
London WC2N 4DF

British Library Cataloguing in Publication Data
Tindall, Gillian
    Rosamond Lehmann
    1. Lehmann, Rosamond—Biography
    2. Novelists, English—20th century—Biography
    I. Title
    823'.912   PR6023.E42Z/

ISBN 0 7011 2706 6
ISBN 0 7011 3946 3 Pbk

Photoset by Rowland Phototypesetting Ltd
Bury St Edmunds, Suffolk
Printed in Great Britain by
Redwood Burn Ltd
Trowbridge, Wiltshire

CONTENTS

ACKNOWLEDGEMENTS

The copyright of all Rosamond Lehmann's novels but one is held by the Society of Authors, and I gratefully acknowledge their permission to quote as necessary from the works and also from an article by Rosamond Lehmann in their publication, *The Author*. To Virago Press, thanks for permission to quote from *A Note in Music*, and also from Janet Watts' Introductions to their paperback editions of the novels – grateful thanks also to Janet Watts herself for this and for permission to quote from the transcript of an interview with Rosamond Lehmann which was subsequently published in *Harper's & Queen*.

My thanks, too, to Panthea Broughton for permission to quote from her dissertation (subsequently published as an article in *South Central Review*, Vol. 1), and to Wiktoria Dorosz for quotation from her thesis. Also to Weidenfeld & Nicolson for a quotation from Sean Day-Lewis's *An English Literary Life*.

I am grateful to King's College Library, Cambridge, for allowing me to quote from papers of Rosamond Lehmann's in their possession, particularly for the unpublished poem, 'The Bay'. My personal thanks also to the librarian, Dr Michael Halls, for his help and encouragement. I have also received informal help from John Lehmann, Elizabeth Jenkins and Lettice Cooper, each of whom was kind enough to let me come and talk about Rosamond's work to them. I am also very grateful to Jenny McKeon for lending me a number of books that have been a help to me.

Many of the above-mentioned formal permissions have

depended, also, on Rosamond Lehmann's own consent. This has been freely given, as of course has her overall consent to my embarking on this project in the first place. She has been most generous with her time, interest and understanding, and I owe a great debt of gratitude to her for allowing me to fulfil a long-term ambition. My thanks too to Carmen Callil of Chatto & Windus for her own encouragement and enthusiasm.

A NOTE FOR THE READER

All page references in this book are to the paperback editions of Rosamond Lehmann's novels, since these are now the most widely obtainable. The publisher of these editions is Virago Press – except in the case of *Dusty Answer* and *The Echoing Grove* where the relevant paperback edition is by Penguin Books.

Where I have quoted from Rosamond Lehmann's work and dots appear, thus . . . this simply indicates her own use of dots in the original, a form of punctuation to which she has been partial. When, however, the dots appear enclosed in square brackets, thus [. . .], this indicates that *I* have made a cut in the text.

This book has no formal index. Readers and reviewers are not, however, invited to take this as a sign of idleness or lack of scholarly attention on the part of myself or my editors: it has been a deliberate decision. The number of books published by Rosamond Lehmann is quite small, each is mentioned over and over again in my text and to most of them whole chapters are effectively devoted. This is not a biography; my text is not concerned with places, people or events so much as with themes. Any index which confined itself, in the traditional way, to concrete items, proper names etc., would be too short and uninformative to be of much use; conversely one which attempted, by some means, to recapitulate the true nature of the book's contents would not make much sense except to someone who had already read the book. I have therefore preferred to set out the contents to each chapter rather more fully than is customary in the Contents, in the hope that this will be of sufficient assistance to any reader wishing to look up a specific book or phase of the author's life.

Gillian Tindall

Another woman writer of Rosamond Lehmann's generation, her long-term friend Lettice Cooper, wrote recently: 'The biography of an author is always a difficult assignment: so much of the real drama lies in the tensions between the writer and his work' (*The PEN*, Autumn 1983).

Yes indeed. For why otherwise would one be writing his biography? The important thing about a writer is that he or she writes – that he or she creates an extraneous world for the imaginations of other people to inhabit. *That* is what is interesting and mysterious about a writer in the final analysis, not what his upbringing was like or whom she has loved or what other famous people they have known. Everything, colourful or apparently commonplace, well publicised or carefully concealed, is ultimately subsumed to the central activity of creative writing.

Yet paradoxically this activity, which almost by definition is a solitary one, is likely to be the writer's least visible occupation. It is the core of the writer's whole existence, even when (as in Rosamond Lehmann's case), it is only intermittently pursued in an active way. But to the outsider this core activity may seem to be taking place in the interstices of life, and centre stage may appear to be occupied by everything else: living, learning, travelling, loving, rearing children, teaching, talking, quarrelling – *being*, and eventually dying. It is understandable when, after the death of the writer, a biographer writes an appreciative, carefully researched, exhaustive ('definitive') study of the writer's life which somehow fails to convey a picture of that person actually writing. It is, however, a pity, and a sign of a problem unsolved – perhaps even unperceived.

But if biographers have a problem, how much greater is the problem of the non-biographer such as myself, who seeks essentially to discuss and illuminate the books of a still living writer rather than to display in detail the life of which they are the product? Much of the work that will be done by an accredited biographer after Rosamond Lehmann's death – the reading of files of letters, the interviewing of survivors, the cataloguing of addresses, events, significant names – would be irrelevant in any case to my particular interest in her. But to pretend, on the other hand, that the general structure and patterns of her personal life have *no* bearing on the appreciation of her novels would be absurd. With all writers there must be some connection between the life and what is created out of that life, even if the connection is a tortuous, oblique or mainly negative one – the writing of what has *not* happened, but could have and has been hoped for or feared, rather than of what has actually taken place. The degree of connection between the novelist and his work varies very much from one novelist to another: some seem to draw the sources of their inspiration from aspects of their life which are not particularly obvious to the onlooker; others are simply good at covering their tracks and disguising what might otherwise seem too personal a statement; others yet again, notoriously, write straight out of their own experience, with a lack of reticence or discretion that shocks those whose own creative powers function differently. One should perhaps add that novelists probably do not really choose the extent to which they reveal or conceal themselves in their work: each person's creative function is as idiosyncratic as his or her dominating ideas and images. Novels are as they are, and their creators have less control of the essential nature of their material than they would like outsiders to suppose.

On the continuum of concealment to revelation, Rosamond Lehmann falls into a curious and interesting category. She herself would agree that elements in her own life have surfaced in all her novels without much conscious attempt at disguise, and that all her central characters have been close to herself and sometimes (in the short stories) totally identified with herself. Yet to assume from this, as too many readers have, that her novels are *romans à cléf* and that you only need to know something about her life and associates to say 'Oh yes – Rollo is X and Rickie is Y and that other book is all about her relationship with celebrated old Z', is a vulgar error of considerable magnitude. Rosamond Lehmann herself has been infuriated by acquaintances and critics – referred to by her as 'spotters' – who indulge in this pastime, but also knows that in a sense she has only herself to blame. The combination of recognisable elements and a highly realistic and convincing surface texture to the books is irresistible to spotters, who appear genuinely to believe that this is how fiction writing works. Snuffling after revealed 'truth', they do not seem to notice that the novels and stories, taken as a whole, do not in fact depict a life anywhere near identical with their author's: the elements of the tales may be taken from fairly patent sources, but meanings of the events are not necessarily the same as in life. In the novels, personalities and situations are woven together in new ways, and therefore create different shapes and messages. When Marghanita Laski writes (in the *London Review of Books*, April 1983) 'with Miss Lehmann's [work] no isolation is possible. With most living novelists [. . .] a first fair test [of excellence] is whether the writer is forgotten by the end of the first few pages. With Miss Lehmann's novels and stories the writer never can be forgotten. Yet this particular test of quality is in her case invalid' – she is near a truth but not quite on it. The truth is that Rosamond Lehmann has the gift of making the reader feel that a novel is a testament of personal reality but the reality in the book is not quite the *same* reality as that in the life. Another woman writer and close contemporary of hers, Elizabeth Jenkins, has said to me: 'Rosamond's life and books are like a carpet – the novels are the right side, where the pattern is clear, and the life is the other side with all the odd threads that don't fit.'

My concern essentially is with the pattern on the carpet.

There are, however, further dimensions to the process of identification – indeed variant meanings in which the word can be used. The reader who automatically identifies Rosamond Lehmann's novels with her life is making one kind of error of simplification, but the reader who identifies the novels with her *own* life is making another, equally tempting error. Rosamond has long been familiar with the kind of reader who writes to her to say 'Oh Miss Lehmann, how did you know? That's my story exactly!' Obviously such a response is heartwarming; it shows that the novel in question has 'worked' on the concrete telling-a-believable-story level on which all novels must initially work. But it is a simplistic response all the same, because it assumes (like the *roman à clef* assumption) that the events of the story told in a novel have an objective existence apart from the telling of them, which is not the case. One of Rosamond Lehmann's great strengths as a novelist has been the way she has conveyed certain timeless and widely experienced human realities within the packaging of fiction. But the packaging is not in fact just packaging, it is part of the expression of the whole; and if the themes she treats have a quality of universality they are nevertheless treated in a way that is highly specific to certain periods, classes and ways of life. The subjective, magpie approach to novel reading – picking out what one feels to be relevant to one's life and preoccupations and ignoring the rest – is widespread and probably inevitable, particularly in youth when fiction is avidly and anxiously used as a guide to fact, but it is a misuse of the novel all the same.

I speak with guilt. Like many women of my generation and the preceding one, I read Rosamond Lehmann's books in youth (in my case in extreme youth – I was about fourteen), found them compelling and convincing, and inevitably formed on them certain impressions of the nature of Life. I felt *Invitation to the Waltz* to be true to reality as I already knew it, and therefore assumed that adult life would be much like its sequel, *The Weather in the Streets* – an assumption, I may say, of dubious utility and one which might be regarded in certain circles as an immoral self-fulfilling prophecy! In my case, it was not so much a matter of 'Oh Miss Lehmann – my story exactly', as 'Oh Miss Lehmann – now I begin to see what my story will be.' I was vaguely surprised when matters turned out otherwise.

This, I suspect, is not an uncommon experience where an apparently realistic writer has made a deep impression on a boy or girl at a formative age. (Some people, indeed, probably spend their whole lives unconsciously seeking or concocting the situations which their earliest significant forays into fiction-reading have stamped deeply upon them. Casualties of literature, they pursue the wraith of literary truth across the recalcitrant wastes of daily living, mistaking, in the process, their own identity and that of others.) In my case, however, there was a further dimension of identification. Since I became a novelist myself at an unsuitably early age (and had indeed been conceitedly convinced that I was one already from the age of about six), Rosamond Lehmann's books helped to form not only my concept of what Life was like but my concept of what novels were like also. And this second influence has continued. For good and ill – and both tend to be present in such processes – her novels have been internalised by me; they are an ineradicable part of my idea of what the novel is and what it may successfully be trying to say. I owe her, therefore, an enormous debt. Yet inevitably, since novelists must grow and change, there has, for me, been an element of undesirable possession also – and hence a need consciously to keep this early, so formative influence at bay by seeking out themes Rosamond never broached or venturing into non-fiction territories to her unknown. I hope she will not take it amiss if I say that the present book is a work of both grateful recognition and deliberate exorcism, and that the two elements are for me inextricably mingled.

CHAPTER I

The place you first thought of

Rosamond Lehmann is a deceptive writer. She seems at times to be offering the reader a view into her own heart when in fact she is offering something subtly alternative, transformed by art and consciousness; and the texture of most of her work is richer and more sophisticated than it may appear. The pattern on the carpet is classic rather than complex or original, but it is woven in a tight and subtle web. Some readers, lulled by the readability and unpretension of her lucid prose, have imagined her work to be 'slight' or 'limited': they are taken in by the art that conceals art, and confuse circumscription of subject-matter with something quite other – a limitation of view.* Rosamond Lehmann's subject matter is certainly circumscribed, in the sense that Jane Austen's was also circumscribed (though their areas of scrutiny were rather different, and in place of Jane Austen's endemic detachment Rosamond Lehmann shows undisguised involvement with her subject matter). Rosamond's territory is the human heart – hardly a minor or esoteric field.

When *The Weather in the Streets* came out in 1936, one reviewer felt he had to warn readers that this novel was 'based upon the assumption that even for certain intelligent, sophisticated persons love can become the most important thing in the world, and upon the further assumption that the novelist may write about the passion of such persons in such a manner as to accept it at their own valuation' (Joseph Wood Krutch, *The Nation*, June 1936). At first sight it is a reasonable

*Though this phrase, 'limitation of view', is also used in another, more technical sense. See Chapter V.

statement, but upon re-reading it becomes apparent that the choice of the patronising word 'assumption' indicates the reviewer's own deficiency and ignorance. He is suggesting by implication that 'intelligent and sophisticated' persons might be expected to have more important things to bother about than love – a highly questionable assumption in itself, and one hardly borne out by the weight of great literature in the world devoted to love and valuing it, indeed, above everything else.

In Rosamond Lehmann's books we are shown people loving, hurting one another, remembering, growing, bringing up children, yearning, reacting to houses, places, landscapes . . . We do not, much, see them working, administering, lecturing, buying and selling, running the country, joining political parties, going to war. To say this is not to imply a limitation but, rather, a close focus on one particular area, with a sense of a wider landscape lying, unspoken but not ignored, beyond the book's confines. Some readers, even, have confused subject matter and treatment to the extent of labelling Rosamond Lehmann 'a romantic novelist', as though a writer who writes about the dark alleys of love rather than the corridors of power were automatically in some sense unserious, unenlightened and escapist. Such labellers have evidently failed to notice that the whole ethos of Lehmann-land runs directly counter to that of the land of Romance, in that her stock-in-trade is not fruitful matings and happy endings but, rather, love misplaced, denied or betrayed – and betrayed not so much by human perfidy as by life, circumstances, time itself. Time, a sense of its passing and of its ultimate power and weight (a sense notably absent from the classic romantic novel) is ever-present in Lehmann-land, and with it much else that is implied rather than made explicit.

She is also one of those writers whose books have evolved with the passing of the years, so that, taken as an ensemble, they form a commentary on her own time, her own journey through the decades. And yet, though the distance covered is considerable, the journey is also in some sense circular: the same images and motifs crop up again and again through the years, though the context in which they are placed changes and the viewpoint changes. When *The Echoing Grove*, generally considered her most ambitious and accomplished novel, was published in 1953, she gave a talk on the BBC in which she said:

. . . While I was tunnelling to find a way through to the end of it I began to feel that, more than any of the others, this novel had something to do with the first I ever wrote. Not the same one in a fresh guise; not even a development from it; but more as if somehow – I cannot explain why – some cycle of experience that had opened when I was a girl was now coming to a close (*The Listener*, March 1953).

I shall return in chapter x to this pregnant statement. For the moment I should like simply to signal that, in the light of it, the title *The Echoing Grove* seems a peculiarly suitable one for the book which she herself recognised as the culmination of her fiction writing. Although very much its own book, tightly and intricately constructed (with, incidentally, a time scheme that turns in on itself, rejecting the linear mode for the circular), it is full of echoes of earlier works, revoicings of permanent preoccupations. Or – to shift the metaphor from the auditory to the visual – it is like a grove of mirrors in which images from earlier books appear and reappear with different modifications and meanings.

Like many, perhaps most novelists, Rosamond Lehmann has a small number of images and situations to which one might apply the word 'obsessional' in that they crop up again and again in her work. It is my belief that these are not only part of the permanent furnishings of the creative mind but are in fact central to the process of creation itself, and this too is a concept to which I shall be returning. The novelist Albert Camus stated the matter even more forcibly, when he wrote in his Preface to *L'Envers et l'Endroit* (1958): 'I know from my own experience that a man's life work is nothing but a long journey to find again, by all the detours of art, the two or three powerful images on which his whole being opened for the first time.' Because of this circularity, this return journey quality in the novelist's odyssey, it is not easy for the critic to know where to start. If the novelist has, indeed, made one long detour back to the place she first thought of, then where does the heart of the pattern lie?

Let us start arbitrarily, therefore, with 'place' in the most concrete sense – the surroundings of childhood. It is not true of all creative writers that the physical surroundings of their childhood become part of their 'powerful images': some, indeed, only find their minds opening when they escape from childhood and its location – but to Rosamond Lehmann the countryside of the Thames Valley where she grew up seems to have become an inner as well as an outer landscape, and also a locale from which she never moved away entirely. Her later years have been spent in London and in Aldeburgh on the east coast, but throughout her childhood, her growing up and her prime decades as a writer, she did not go far for long from the Buckinghamshire-Berkshire-Oxfordshire triangle of her upbringing. Her one removal to a quite other part of England – her brief marriage to Leslie Runciman (1924-7) was spent in Newcastle – seems to have been traumatic for geographical reasons as well as for others. Her own sense of desolation in the alien, chilly north is voiced through the central character of *A Note in Music* (1930), and indeed the book was written when she had already escaped from that place and that marriage. Elsewhere in that and other novels an enormous responsiveness to the beauty and intricacy of southern England and its climate is frequently manifest. Events are orchestrated by the seasons. And the river Thames, or another anonymous river that seems to derive from it, haunts her novels, lying there round a bend in the road, receiving the characters at key moments in the plots, evoking memories, linking past and future. Water is one of Rosamond Lehmann's primary and most powerful images.

She was born on the Thames at Bourne End, in Buckinghamshire, not far in one direction from suburban Maidenhead and in the other from still countrified Cookham, where Stanley Spencer painted his detailed, obsessive landscapes: his countryside is hers also. Today Bourne End is an overgrown commuter district, a 'village' still only by courtesy and British rural sentimentality: although it is technically within London's Green Belt, infilling along the main roads has destroyed any sense of rural unity. When Rosamond's father, R. C. Lehmann, built a house there near the river in 1895, the place still gave an impression of country peace and distance from London, although in fact the suburban railway had come, and with it people like R. C. Lehmann who were themselves unwitting harbingers of the destruction to follow. Fieldhead, the house he built, and enlarged a few years later when he married, was slightly rambling, elegant in the post-William Morris, neo-Queen Anne style then favoured by the artistic and the sophisticated, and stood in several acres of ground with its own access to a boat-house on the Thames. It would have been a spacious and pleasant gentleman's house by the standards of that or any other era: today the modern mind gapes in wonder over the fact that, at the turn of the century, a man of letters who was merely 'comfortably off', not conspicuously wealthy, should have been able to afford such a home, in such a location, built to his own tastes, plus the staff to run it – about six indoor servants, four gardeners and a coachman.

R. C. Lehmann, a scholar and a noted athlete (oarsman), was descended from a cosmopolitan line of musicians and painters who came from Vienna* earlier in the nineteenth century; and also, on his mother's side, from Robert Chambers, of the *Encyclopaedia*, a towering figure of nineteenth-century literary life. At Cambridge, R. C. Lehmann founded *Granta*; he was at one time editor of the *Daily News* and a permanent member of the round table at *Punch*. He took over the editorship of *Punch* in the occasional absences of the editor, Owen Seamans, and for a brief period was a Liberal M.P. He published a number of popular and very accomplished books of light verse. His New England wife, of 'true blue' Puritan *Mayflower* stock, was much younger than him; he had met her while on a visit to the United States when he was coaching at Harvard and she, as an ex-Radcliffe girl, was teaching the daughters of the Peabody family, with whom he stayed in Boston. Rosamond Lehmann has described him to me as 'a difficult man with a frightful temper' but also as 'so handsome, clever, literary, musical – everything . . . we all adored him'. The pleasant house by the river received a stream of cultivated and sometimes eminent visitors; R. C. Lehmann's three daughters – Rosamond was the second, Beatrix the youngest – and his son John, who was the baby of the family, were born into propitious and nurturing circumstances.

These were also highly sheltered circumstances. The girls were not sent to school but were 'educated at home' in the by then rather old-fashioned phrase: in fact the Lehmann parents had built a brick pavilion in the grounds of the house and this, for a number of years, became a small and exclusive school for their daughters, which children of suitable neigh-

---

*The family were of Jewish origins, but no longer considered themselves Jewish. Despite Rosamond Lehmann's apparent choice of a Jewish identity for herself as 'Rebecca Landon', the autobiographical narrator of *The Ballad and the Source*, she grew up entirely at home in the world of the British upper classes, regarding herself as 'entirely English'.

bours also attended. Their education was further augmented by foreign nursery governesses and, later, by specialised tutors. Rosamond had the run of her father's library, which seems to have provided her with a good background of nineteenth-century literature but little twentieth-century. When *Dusty Answer* was published in 1927 some critics assumed her to be a follower of Virginia Woolf, but in fact she has said that almost the only modern woman novelist she had then read was May Sinclair – a writer, incidentally, likely to reinforce a private, home-based, rather solitary view of life. It was not till she went to Girton at the age of seventeen-and-a-half that she left home in any sense, and her first, shrinking reaction to the ugliness and noise of communal life there among a horde of girls from varying backgrounds manifests itself in *Dusty Answer*. It was then – in 1919 – still rather unusual for a girl from Rosamond's kind of family to go to college: she and her elder sister Helen only went at their American mother's insistence. Mrs Lehmann, coming herself from a world where a college education was already the norm for well-to-do young women, had read History at Radcliffe and had achieved the highest academic honours ever achieved by a woman in that subject. R. C. Lehmann, at first mildly resistant to the idea of his daughters becoming 'blue stockings', was finally won over by the charm of the Mistress of Girton.

Rosamond was not indulged as a child – neither in England nor in America at that date did well-educated people indulge their children – but she was reared in surroundings of beauty and comfort, and remained permanently aware of such things and vulnerable to their absence. Today, her girlhood home still stands intact. The tulip-shaped *art nouveau* leading on the glass doors in the entrance hall is still there; so is the pale stained-glass window at the turn of the stairs, so are the elegant brass bell-pushes and finger-plates on the doors, so are the rafters of R. C. Lehmann's big library and the white railings of the wide balconies outside the first floor bedrooms. To the reader of the short stories, in particular, it is all wonderfully recognisable: in this library Rosamond Lehmann, alias Rebecca Landon or Ellison,* is sitting with her father when Wyatt the shepherd comes to tell them his wife has died in hospital ('The Gipsy's Baby'†, 39). In those nurseries and in that spacious garden and shrubbery the children ranged like royalty in their own kingdom, in that drawing-room Rebecca's cool mother sat reading the emotion-laden letter from Mrs Jardine which opens the events of *The Ballad and the Source*. But nurseries and drawing-room are now occupied alike by single beds with candlewick covers, divided from one another by curtains, and in the library (where some of R. C. Lehmann's books still stand on the shelves) wheeled chairs are lined up for tea. The house, much too big today for any private occupant, has become an old people's home. The large garden has been divided up into separate building lots; many of the big, old beeches, wellingtonias and cedars have been preserved, but they stand cut off from the original establishment, stretching their boughs over runs of 'estate type' houses. The shrubbery and vegetable gardens are gone completely. But the door that led from this Eden into the side lane, the small door the children used when they wanted to make forays into another world, that of the Wyatts and the other cottagers, is still here. The lane, gravelled, is still much as it must have been seventy years ago. However, the cottages, cleaned, painted and prettified, now have different and more monied occupants. The world has invaded the walled Bourne End home. And that world itself has also changed so that many of the old values and meanings no longer apply.

Thus, quickly and inevitably, the importance of class in the

---

*The surname varies with some inconsistency from one story to another, but the family is clearly the same.

†The first story in the collection entitled *The Gipsy's Baby and other stories*.

world which produced Rosamond Lehmann and her novels rears its head. One should not underestimate its real and deep significance or try, with misplaced post-1945 ideas of democracy and good taste, to gloss it over and pretend that it is a mere detail. John Lehmann remarked to me that 'Class is everywhere in English fiction before the Second World War', and that is because it was everywhere in English life at that time. An accurate perception of class background is integral to Rosamond Lehmann's view of people; it is an important part of her sense of what they mean to one another. Rollo and Rickie (to instance only the central male characters of her two most successful novels) are individuals, but they are also very much representatives of a particular social class; so, in a different way, is Tom, the husband in *A Note in Music*. The Fyfes in *Dusty Answer* are imbued (as are the Spencers in *Invitation to the Waltz* and *The Weather in the Streets*) with a class glamour as well as a glamour of another kind for the young Judith. And, at the other end of the scale, you cannot properly appreciate that rich and deceptively inconclusive story, 'The Red-Haired Miss Daintreys', unless you are prepared to understand that what fascinates the Ellison children about the Daintreys' middle-class world of genteel commercialism is that it is, to them, just as exotic and revelatory an environment in its way as the world of the Wyatts. As for the Wyatts, they stand for a whole other universe, as romantic and intimidating to the young Ellisons as the slums of London were to Michael Fane in Compton Mackenzie's *Sinister Street*, that earlier saga of Youth confronting Real Life.

At the bottom of the lane that ran between our garden wall and the old row of brick cottages lived the Wyatt family. Their dwelling stood by itself, with a decayed vegetable patch in front of it, and no grass, and not a flower; and behind it a sinister shed with broken palings, and some old tyres, kettles and tin basins, and a rusty bicycle frame, and a wooden box on wheels; and potato peelings, bones, fish heads, rags and other fragments strewn about. The impression one got as one passed was of mud and yellowing cabbage stalks, and pools of water that never drained away. After a particularly heavy rainfall there was water all round the door and even inside, on the floor of the kitchen. Cursing but undaunted, wearing a battered cloth cap on her head, Mrs Wyatt drove it out again and again, year after year, with a mop. It was an insanitary cottage with no damp course, mean little windows in rotting frames and discoloured patches on the walls ('The Gipsy's Baby', 1).

Thus the story begins. Mrs Wyatt, who gives birth to a baby a year, is 'a small crooked-hipped exhausted slattern with a protruding belly and black rotten stumps of teeth. Her beautiful wild eyes were of a fanatical blue, and when she fixed them on you they seemed to pierce beyond the back of your skull. Her face was worn away to bone and stretched skin, and in the middle of each hollow cheek was a stain of rose, like one live petal left on a dead flower' (9-10). All her numerous family are plain, with 'flat, broad, shallow skulls' and 'sparse, mousish hair' except for one girl, Chrissie, a diminutive, gipsy-ish creature:

Her brow was knobby, over-developed, disquieting with its suggestion of precocity, of a fatal excess. She frowned perpetually in a fierce worried way, and her prominent mouth would not shut properly. It made a sharp, rather vicious looking circle of red round her tiny white teeth. Some charitable person had given her a frock of black and scarlet plaid that fitted tightly to her miniature form and gave her the enhanced reality, or the unreality, of a portrait of a child [. . .] The frock did get more and more exiguous; but Chrissie did not grow much, or fill out at all. Against the dun background of her sister and brothers she was isolated and set off: as if her mother's degenerating flesh and bone had combined with the nondescript clay of her father to produce the rest; but Chrissie had been conceived from that bright splash of living blood in her mother's cheek (10–11).

Three of the Wyatts, including Chrissie, manage to insinuate themselves into the Ellison nursery for a constrained tea party, and Chrissie it is who later spreads a wild, baseless, envious story in the lane that 'It was horrible, awful in there anyway, a kind of torture chamber; nobody was allowed to talk, *not even to smile* at the tea-table' (33). Chrissie it is also who eventually, when her mother has died with 'brain fever' after giving birth to yet another baby, spreads the information in the local elementary school that gipsies have left a dead, naked baby boy on the Common under the bramble bushes. This is the 'gipsy's baby' of the title. The local police are called in. But there is, it eventually transpires, no baby: Chrissie has made the whole thing up.

We never saw Chrissie again. The problems of her disgrace, her punishment, her future – all were kept from us; and even the know-alls of the lane were more or less in the dark about her destination when she vanished from the village.

We knew that our mother, ever combining prompt with humanitarian action, had taken charge of Chrissie's case. We did venture to ask Isabel [the Nurse] whether it was true that Chrissie had been sent to a reformatory, but she said sharply, stuff and nonsense: Chrissie had gone right away to live with some kind people who loved her, and who would give her a mother's care and perhaps adopt her if she mended her ways and tried to be a good girl [. . .] So we knew that something impressive had been accomplished and that our parents were paying for it (52–3).

So, although the dead baby is a fantasy, it is as if the gipsy-ish Chrissie herself had died and been translated to another sphere. Most of the remaining Wyatt children are sent to 'the Institution' while the eldest, Maudie, remains at home caring for the youngest, taking on the traditional rôle of her class and sex:

There was a neighbour, Mrs Smith the washerwoman, who was kind. Once I ran down with a message from Nurse to ask her to wash the nursery sofa cover in a hurry and Maudie was there, sitting slumped in a kitchen chair, drinking a cup of tea, silent, grimy, greasy, her hair screwed and scraped up into a bun with huge hairpins. She had put it up, I suppose, to mark the fact that she was now a woman: one of a thousand, thousand anonymous ones who bear their sex, not at the unconscious, fluid, fructifying centre, as women who are loved bear it and are upborne by it; but as it were extraneously, like a deformity, a hump on their backs, weighing them down, down, towards the sterile stones of the earth (45).

There were real Wyatts in Rosamond Lehmann's childhood, but they did not in fact live in the lane near the house, or come to tea. We meet them – the essential Wyatts in a marginally different guise – elsewhere in her work. In *Invitation to the Waltz* (1932), in another village like Bourne End, the sweep's children appear:

Intensely serious they were, hoarse, wary; forlorn as a group strayed from another world and clinging defensively together. Their eyes were sharp, bright, hard, rats' eyes above high sharp cheek bones, their lips long, thin and flat, their skulls narrow and curiously knobbed. They didn't look like other people's children. They had hardly any hair; and under-sized frames with square high shoulders, almost like hunchbacks, and frail legs; and they were enclosed in large trailing ragged coats, swathes of trouser, strange adult boots that clapped and flapped as they ran. Regularly once a year the new baby became the old baby. There seemed no warning, but there it was – another weevil, blanched, shrivelled, perfectly silent, carried forth from the cottage triumphantly among them for an airing, as ants convey an egg [. . .] Though haggard, sagging, crooked, with chaotic teeth and hair, Mrs Wainwright was by no means daunted or depressed, and frequently was heard to declare that she wouldn't be without one of them. Often of an afternoon, when not actually in the throes of childbirth, she abandoned her unprofitable household cares, put on a spirited hat with feathers, and took them all for a walk. Merrily the squeaking pram trundled, brimming with children [. . .] When they came back towards dark the pram was heavier. The little ones lay softer. Sometimes it was hen feathers, sometimes rabbit fur . . . Mrs Wainwright was said to be a gipsy (75–7).

So the idea that, behind the alien world of the Wyatts-Wainwrights lies a still more exotic and alarming one, that of the gipsies, hovers in this tale too. But in *Invitation to the*

Waltz no further use is made of the family except to taunt the eighteen-year-old Olivia – 'And cackles, rude hoots and howls pursued her until she was out of sight. Really, it didn't do to try to be nice to the little Wainwrights' – and, though there is an apparent Chrissie's mother, there is no Chrissie. The Ur-Wyatts, then, are from life. But Chrissie, the heart and point of 'The Gipsy's Baby', is a creation from some other realm of the writer's fertile mind.

Mr Wyatt's arrival, in the short story, at the french windows of the library the evening his wife has died, giving Rebecca her first sight of unassuageable adult grief, also has its genesis in a real event. Rosamond Lehmann recalls Mr Moody, their coachman-turned-chauffeur, appearing on the lawn in similar apocalyptic guise to announce to his concerned employer a bereavement. But it was not his wife who had died but his small daughter – of diphtheria. The event is described in Rosamond Lehmann's memoir *The Swan in the Evening* (1967):

The tragedy shattered us one and all. Julia [Nurse] sobbed in the nursery, harrowing herself, us, the nurse-maid, with recollections of the times she'd called it a sin and a shame, the way Moody spoilt that child ... Could Wilma have been taken as a judgement? [. . .] The worst was the sight of my father weeping in the library [. . .]

We were all severely shaken; but we all recovered; all but Moody. More than once I have heard it said that we are never given more to bear than we are able to bear. It is not true, in my experience. Some of us cannot bear what we are given. Moody was one of these [. . .] Only one more memory [of him] returns. Again I am sitting beside him on the box and being driven through the purlieus of Marlow on my way to a tea-party. It is a slum street of poor low houses, and from the door of one of them a little girl runs into the road, almost brushes the wheel, darts back again. She is a ragged child and very dirty and has no shoes or stockings (barefoot boys and girls could still be seen when I was a child). Presently Moody says in a stone voice: '*She'll* live. Nobody wants her but she'll live – grow up to be a -- and one that has every care, that's the apple of your eye, that you'd lay down your life for gladly . . .'

Silence again (25–6).

The desperately bereaved working man – the amoral ragged girl darting dangerously across their path – the image of the dead child . . . The essential elements of the drama in 'The Gipsy's Baby' all seem to be here in the recollection, not knit as in the story but in a dispersed, fragmented, real life form. Is it fanciful to suggest that that small, ragged girl, momentarily glimpsed and then enshrined in memory, was one of the elements that, over thirty years later, went into the making of Chrissie?

We shall revisit this and related images again. Dead children haunt Rosamond Lehmann's novels, not obtrusively or even dramatically as in Victorian works, but persistently, pervasively, taking various different forms, part of the hidden agenda of the imagery as much as of the overt text. I would be tempted to say 'ominously', were it not that that term begs questions about time, pre-recognition and the nature of reality that lie well beyond the scope of this study. When writing about Mr Moody's child Wilma, Rosamond Lehmann adds: 'Not till close on half a century later, when I in my turn suffered the cruellest and seemingly most unnatural of all human bereavements, did I think of her again, and of her father, who must have joined her long ago [. . .]' (29).

Wilma Moody just disappeared, from the point of view of the Lehmann children: death was not made visible, not faced as such: 'when she [Julia] returned from paying her last respects, she conjured before our eyes the picture of an unimaginable Wilma in her little coffin, clasping a bunch of forget-me-nots [. . .] She had become a little angel' (25). But a few pages later in *The Swan in the Evening* Rosamond Lehmann evokes the deeply disturbing memory of the 'hospital for birds' she maintained in a garden playhouse. She used to rescue stunned or agitated birds from the fruit nets during the gardener's lunch hour, and carry them off to her play house and bed them down

so that their mothers can come for them. Whether or no something of this nature does occur, at all events, when I return a few hours later, or perhaps the next morning, the hospital bed is empty. But one day I extricate a young blackbird caught by the neck. As soon as I cut him down his head sags; his wing is broken too. The case seems grave, so I wrap him completely in cotton wool before placing him in the box and tip-toeing away. Then oblivion, based probably upon foreboding, supervenes. Days pass before I next visit my kennel. The ball of cotton wool lies as I left it, motionless . . . no, not absolutely motionless . . . There seems a sort of pervasive stir or tremor . . . I open it, drop it, aghast; take to my heels.

  After that, my house stands vacant in perpetuity (33–4).

Dead child – dead bird: bird whose mother has failed to 'come for it' – mother who has failed to protect and nurture her child in spite of love: we meet this symbolism again. In *A Note in Music* the childless central character, Grace Fairfax, has a stillborn baby; later she tries, but fails, to rear a mongrel puppy bought in the market; later again, on an escapist holiday into her childhood countryside of the south, she makes an attempt to rescue a young, injured swallow. It will not eat the crumbs she sprinkles for it, but it looks at her with a bright, unglazed eye until finally, at sunset, it tucks its head beneath its wing and goes to sleep in her lap –

She carried it up and set it, lapped in unstirring infant sleep, in the fold of a woollen scarf by the open sill. She woke before dawn and discerned it still motionless there, dark and round as a ball. When next she woke the sun was up, and all the birds were calling; and it had flown away.

  She took this for a message, a happy omen. For the first time, she told herself, she had touched something to save, not to destroy it (192).

But the omen is an illusion. Weeks later, on

The day of her departure, walking for the last time in the garden, she saw, half-hidden in the flower-bed beneath her bedroom window, the draggled skeleton of a young swallow.

So it had been there all the time, waiting for her: it had dropped down, of course, and had been broken, and never flown away. There was no winged life existing through her care (227).

Anyone who has ever wanted a child and not conceived one will recognise the significance of the time-lapse element in Grace's disappointment. It comes as a relief to record that Rosamond Lehmann, unlike her rather too shadowy and unsatisfactory Grace Fairfax, made a permanent escape from the north into a second marriage in which she bore two children, who were a source of great joy and fulfilment for her, whatever the dark future held.

In some women the nurturing, maternal impulses only de-velop in response to the presence of an actual baby. In others, they seem to have been there from the start. Thus, with the ratiocinative image of the child, or child-substitute, living or dead, we are at Rosamond Lehmann's end and also at her beginning. A pattern, potentially, was always there. Writers dream and invent their future as well as meeting it, practising already in childhood on the themes, the 'two or three powerful images', that are going to be explored and recreated again and again in their future novels.

'The Red-Haired Miss Daintreys', as well as being a story about class and sexuality and the mysterious *otherness* of alien people's lives, is also a story about memory and writing and the relation between the two. Indeed creative writing, and its 'essential storing house' in the mind of the writer, is the topic with which Rosamond Lehmann begins her tale – a shade didactically for her:

I am surprised when authors have perfectly clear plans about the novels they are going to write; and I find it dismaying, for more reasons than one, to have the projected contents related to me, at length and in rational sequence. I would be more encouraged by such an answer, given in rather a hostile and depressed way, as: It is about some people; and if the author could bear to pursue the subject and mention any of the images and symbols haunting his mind – if he spoke for instance of a fin turning in a waste of waters, of the echo in the caves, of an empty room, shuttered under dust sheets, of an April fall of snow, of music from the fair at night, of the burnt-out shell of a country house, that woman seen a moment from the bus stop, brushing long dark hair – I should feel that something was afoot. Writers should stay more patiently at the centre and suffer themselves to be worked upon. Later on, when they finally emerge towards the circumference they may have written a good novel about love or war or the class struggle. Or they may not have written a good novel at all.

But this is a far cry from the four red-haired Miss Daintreys [. . .] (*The Gipsy's Baby*, 58).

CHAPTER II

The house on the hill

Locations are often more persistent in a writer's mind than characters. In Rosamond's Lehmann's first novel, the highly acclaimed *Dusty Answer* (1927), the Lehmann family are absent: Judith, the central character, is an only child. But the house in which she is brought up is clearly a version of Fieldhead, the Lehmann home, with the Thames as a constant presence. Moreover, the 'house next door', which crops up in the first line of the book and whose inmates are to provide most of the novel's action, *is*, according to Rosamond Lehmann, the actual house next door, Abney, which, like Fieldhead, still stands but is converted to other uses. It is 'next door' in an expansive, upper-class sense, for the lane – the Wyatt lane – actually divides its garden from Fieldhead, and subsequent building has hemmed it in. But it remains an attractive, rambling house, probably late Georgian in origin, with substantial Victorian additions. During the Lehmann family's childhood it was occupied by Arthur Hammersley and his talented, attractive, second wife Violet. Its lawns, unlike those of Fieldhead, run straight down to the river, and indeed in *Dusty Answer* the magic of the river seems more the property of the magic, elusive, Fyfes than of Judith's own family. Their place in her mental landscape is delineated in the first paragraph:

When Judith was eighteen, she saw that the house next door, empty for years, was getting ready again. Gardeners mowed and mowed, and rolled and rolled the tennis-court; and planted tulips and forget-me-nots in the stone urns that bordered the lawn at the river's edge. The ivy's long fingers were torn away from the windows, and the solid grey stone front made prim and trim. When the blinds went up

and the familiar oval mirror-backs once more stared from the bedroom windows it seemed as if the long time of emptiness had never
been, and that the next-door children must still be there with their
grandmother, – mysterious and thrilling children who came and
went, and were all cousins except two who were brothers, and all
boys except one, who was a girl; and who dropped over the peach-tree
wall into Judith's garden with invitations to tea and hide-and-seek (7).

There we have already, exposed with admirable ease and
economy, what anyone familiar with other books by the
author will recognise as a quintessential Lehmann situation.
Judith, whose home background is in fact no less moneyed or
cultured than that of the Fyfes', nevertheless feels something
of a wistful outsider and longs to be more closely incorporated
into their family circle. This feeling dates from childhood, and
childhood has forged bonds there. But, although when the
novel opens Judith is still a prisoner of the long, sheltered,
upper-class childhood of the period, in fact time has moved
on. She reflects that 'They would be grown up and smart, with
friends from London; and she still had her hair down and
wore black cotton stockings, and blushed wildly, hopelessly,
eternally when addressed in public. It would be appalling to
meet them again, remembering so much they had certainly
forgotten' (9).

More crucially, the First World War has supervened:

In truth all was different now. The grandmother had died soon after
she heard Charlie was killed. He had been her favourite, her darling
one. He had, astoundingly, married the girl Mariella when they were
both nineteen, and he just going to the front. He had been killed
directly, and some months afterwards Mariella had had a baby (7).

So the four years of war lie there, cutting off past from
present, firmly 'over' now but in another sense never over.
The invisible presence of this war haunts the background of
this novel as it does all the novels, including the one written
long after all the others and published in 1976 (*A Sea-Grape*

Tree). As a trauma, and as a perceived engine of social change for the generation of which Rosamond Lehmann belongs, the war is almost impossible to overestimate. See – just one example among many – *The Ballad and the Source* (1944), a book in which another nearby big house, and another family of parentless children in the care of their grandmother, exercise a fascination for the central narrator, here Rebecca Landon:

As the war dragged on, the letters grew fewer. I think it was towards the autumn of 1916 that they ceased [. . .] For us, too, life had taken on a fixed melancholy. My father had set out without complaint upon his slow heart-rending journey into the shadows*. Here, there, on every hand, inchmeal, the view beyond the windows of our home contracted, clouded. Our friends' brothers, the big boys who had partnered us in the polka, Sir Roger, the Lancers at pre-war Christmas parties, were being killed in Flanders, at Gallipoli; were being torpedoed and drowned at sea. An unrelenting diet of maize and lentils brought us out in spots, chilblains caused us to limp, the bathwater stopped being hot at night (219).

The surviving Fyfes – Julian, Martin, Mariella and Rodney – are thus inescapably *post-war*, with all that that term of suppressed nostalgia and grief implied for the two decades before another war came along and rendered it obsolete. Julian is a survivor in the literal sense, one of the earliest of a long line of literary stereotypes, embittered by their own survival from the holocaust and the death there of their favourite brother, cousin or friend. Mariella has been helplessly affected by the war, indeed forced into premature motherhood by its dislocating urgency; Martin and Rodney were presumably too young to fight in it, and are affected by that also. They, and Judith, are becoming adult in a world where the old rules and assumptions have been broken: a new, bleak freedom is all around.

In a similar, if less dramatic way, the irreparable changes

*R. C. Lehmann contracted Parkinson's Disease at this time and died of it many years later.

and losses of the war are part of the background assumptions to *Invitation to the Waltz* (1932), which is also set in a Bourne End-style hamlet in the Home Counties somewhere north-west of London — at any rate it is reached via Paddington and even, like Bourne End, has nearby paper mills. There live the Curtises, whose younger daughter Olivia will be the main protagonist of both this novel and another in a different setting, *The Weather in the Streets* (1936). The scene is set of a peaceful country village, with mills (the family business) in the nearby town, but within a few paragraphs we are told:

But times are changing. It is the year 1920; and James, last fruit of a late marriage, is but seven years old. Victim of overwork during the war, his father has retired at sixty in poor health; a gap yawns for the first time in the line of direct succession. Distant relatives and relatives by marriage and such as are not relatives all assume authority. Besides, nowadays who knows what boys will grow up to be, to want or not to want? [. . .] Where are the young men? The mould is the same, but it is cracked: the flavour is strange; it dissipates itself; is spent. Perhaps the last James will never have a car and go to and from Tulverton mills (2).

Mr Curtis is considerably older than his efficient wife; they have two daughters and the young son: the family thus bears a close superficial resemblance to the Lehmann family. Indeed the boy James is obviously modelled on John Lehmann as a child (one of John Lehmann's disconcertingly neat childhood poems is attributed to him); and Rosamond Lehmann has told me that, in portraying the elder sister Kate in this book, her own older sister Helen was in her mind as a physical model. But such resemblances should not be over-interpreted. There is one absolute and significant difference between the Curtis and the Lehmann families, and that is that they do not come — quite — from the same social level. The Lehmanns were, as I have said, a culturally distinguished family and, at any rate in Rosamond's earlier childhood, extremely well-off. They were, indeed, exactly the sort of slightly glamorous family

which *other* people admired. When *Dusty Answer* was published, the critic L. A. G. Strong (who was an Oxford don)
wrote to the author:

One thing about it which particularly captured me was the way it
chimed with my memories of Fieldhead. The few days I spent there
have been a tremendous landmark in my life, and dated a good many
things for me. You and your elder sister were a good deal in the light
of the Fyfes to me – except that you were wonderfully friendly and
welcoming, not exclusive! But you did seem to me a different order
of beings: I felt bucolic, a lout, but a very happy lout: and those days
are one of my best memories.

But the Curtises are merely the declining remnant of a
Victorian mill-owning family. Their house, described in some
detail in *Invitation to the Waltz*, is a solid, Victorian family
house, big enough to have two or three servants and a school
room, but it lacks glamour. Both Kate and Olivia have a secret,
desperate feeling that they never go anywhere or do anything,
and that such attractive, upper-class young men as the neigh-
bourhood does possess are in some indefinable way beyond
their ken. Hence the enormous importance for both of them
assumed by the dance at the neighbouring Big House, home
of Sir John and Lady Spencer, which forms the centre-piece
to this brief, wonderfully engaging novel.

The Big House, however, did have counterparts in Rosamond Lehmann's own girlhood, and, like Fieldhead and
Abney, one possible original for it may still be seen today.
This is Taplow Court near Maidenhead. John Lehmann, who
told me this, referred to it with a smile as 'the house on the
hill', and the name seems apposite, partly because Taplow
Court does indeed stand upon a rise above the river Thames
which has been a place of habitation (and burial) since Celtic
times; partly because a house of this kind figures in *Invitation
to the Waltz* and *The Weather in the Streets* as a kind of House
Beautiful which the guest is privileged to enter; and partly

because a quite other but equally significant house in *The Ballad and the Source* (The Priory, where Mrs Jardine lives) is placed like a fairy-tale dwelling at the top of a green hill.

Taplow Court was the family home of Lord Desborough – the Grenfell family. Lord Desborough was R. C. Lehmann's closest local friend. Rebuilt in the 1850s on the site of an older house, it stands on its terrace of land in impressive, homogeneous Victorian-tudor. Readers of *Invitation to the Waltz* who manage to penetrate inside it (today it is the headquarters of the Plessey Corporation) will have the impression of recognising the gravel sweep of the drive, the galleried hall, the great staircase, the long ballroom which could be made out of opening the double doors between several other rooms, the masculine retreat where Rollo takes Olivia to talk to Sir John, the terrace on which they have previously encountered one another:

[. . .] Fresh arrivals came pouring in from the outer hall, swiftly controlled and conducted as sex demanded by darting, glistening young footmen – green lizards with gilt button scales (153–4).

. . . they [Kate and Olivia] drifted on apprehensively and came to a halt just inside the ballroom. The band had just stopped. Groups, including several young men in hunting coats, stood about the room. And there was Marigold, running towards them, swinging a little basket full of programmes with silk cords and tiny pencils of different colours, wearing an extraordinary and fascinating frock of deep cream spotted net reaching to her ankles, high-waisted, with little puffed sleeves and rows and rows of frills round the skirt, and a sash of water-green satin tied at the back in a fly-away bow. A frock that made other frocks insipid, commonplace, unenterprising. She wore a wreath of green leaves in her fair, curly hair; and her face, that sketch of a few lines, was to-night lightly accentuated by the colours of her excitement – the blurred rose on her cheekbones, the deeper blue of her eyes, the black of their dilated pupils.

'Hallo!' Her voice was pitched high, unlike her mother's, but it had the same penetrating ring. 'Have a programme.' She shook her basket, and all the pink, blue, green and yellow pencils jumped and twisted on their cords. 'Here – green for Kate, yellow for Olivia. How are you enjoying yourselves? Isn't it fun? Rollo's come. Isn't he gorgeous?'

They agreed enthusiastically, looking with diffidence towards the piano, over which her brother leaned in the midst of a laughing group, strumming with one finger and joking with the pianist. Rollo was not for them (156-8).

In fact Rollo *is* for Olivia, but in another place and time – a possibility unperceived by her in that novel, and only very vaguely perceived at that point by Rosamond Lehmann, whose *The Weather in the Streets* still lay several years in the future.

The period elements – the programmes, the surface formality of the whole proceedings, the chilling post-war fact that Kate and Olivia have been asked to 'bring partners with them' (they manage one between them – a dreary godson of Mrs Curtis) – are obvious, yet the emotions the two girls are experiencing on the brink of this social ordeal are of all time: will I be liked, am I pretty enough, is my dress all right, will the young man I dream of ask me to dance – will *anyone* ask me to dance – will I even be *noticed*? Indeed such emotions transcend classes too: the reader need not come from Rosamond Lehmann's own background – or Olivia's – to recognise and respond to what is being expressed. Like Judith in *Dusty Answer*, the seventeen-year-old Olivia feels an outsider, excluded from a world of people who all know each other and what to say to each other. Marigold, the daughter of the house, is seen through a haze of Olivia's sense of inferiority: once a schoolroom friend, she is now the quintessential Other Girl with whom the men all fall in love, impregnably happy and at ease, running off to her own set. Rollo, an Army officer, resplendent this evening in hunting pink, is the quintessential glamorous older brother and only son of the house. Only? Yes, for the other son, Guy, was (of course) killed in the war. The fact is only briefly and belatedly alluded to in *Invitation to the Waltz*: in this book the reality of war is represented, rather, by a man blinded in the trenches with whom Olivia dances, and who sets her lucid, undisciplined imagination going. But in *The Weather in the Streets*, which takes place ten years later, the dead Guy is more firmly present, symbol of a way of life that has gone and will not return however much time goes by. With an ironic, shorthand romanticism, the loss of him is catalogued:

The charcoal head of him as a boy, by Sargent: an Edwardian dream-child with romantic hair, and one of those long necks in an open cricket shirt [. . .]
But he died for England: going over the top, at the head of his men, shot through the heart . . . All as it should be. And they'd done what could be done: worn white for mourning; put a memorial window in the church; collected his letters and poems and all the tributes to him, had them printed for private circulation. All bore witness – nurses, governesses, schoolmasters, broken-hearted friends – all said the same: gay, brilliant, winning, virtuous, brave Guy: pattern of the eldest son . . . (87).

And immediately at this point in the novel a living young man is referred to, a cousin, Archie, unsatisfactory, workshy, perhaps a drunk – we have met him in *Invitation to the Waltz*. And later in the second novel it transpires that Rollo himself feels that Guy was, in some sense, better than himself and that that was why he was killed. The message is clear.

Similarly, in *Dusty Answer*, it is Charlie who has died before the story proper even starts, because he was the one to whom Judith, as a child, had been most romantically drawn, and to whom Julian, his brother, was the most attached:

An utter misery showed for a moment in his face, and he paused before adding: 'And no portrait. Do you remember him?'
'Of course.' Her throat ached with tears. 'He was the most beautiful person – '
'Yes he was. A *spring* of beauty. He didn't care about that, you know, in spite of what people said. His physical brilliance somehow

obscured his character, I think, made it difficult to judge. But he had a very simple heart.' (61)

We are here again, although the location is different, very much in Grenfell country. Two of Lord Desborough's three sons were killed in the war, one of them being the poet Julian Grenfell, cut off at the age of twenty-six. (Tragically, the third son was also to die after the war, in a motor smash.) Their memorial is at Taplow Court, in the gardens. Julian Grenfell's best known poem, 'Into Battle', is inscribed upon it.

In an article she wrote for the journal of the Society of Authors in 1983, Rosamond said: 'I had it lodged in my subconscious mind [as a young woman] that the wonderful unknown young man whom I should have married had been killed in France, along with all the other wonderful young men; so that any other suitor – and quite a few uprose – would be a secondary substitute, a kind of simulacrum.'

Where indeed are the young men? Evidently that question from the opening passages of *Invitation to the Waltz* does not simply reflect the post-war uncertainties of entrenched families like the Curtises or yet Olivia and Kate's rooted, dateless, girlhood *angst* that no one will ever want to marry them. It has a deeper significance in the context both of Rosamond Lehmann's life and of her chosen themes. There is in fact a 'wonderful young man' figure that moves through her books. But he is not a husband.

When *The Echoing Grove* came out in 1953, the novelist Simon Raven wrote in *The Listener* (9 April): 'Rosamond Lehmann's basic theme has always been the traumas of love . . . a theme coeval with human life, that of the woman whose love goes bad on her. In this, there is nothing uncommon; what is uncommon is Miss Lehmann's sense of the elegiac, of the tears of things and the magical way she gives expression to that sense.'

But just why does the love go bad? Is it because, at some level, Lehmann-woman, passionately as she loves, does not herself think that her loved one is the right one or that this situation can last? It is as if the unseen war had killed not only godlike men who could love and be loved unreservedly but faith in the nature of permanence as well. In novel after novel love brings pain with it, not because it 'goes bad' but because it is somehow doomed from the start – unacknowledged, clandestine, unsuitable or even outrageous. From *Dusty Answer*, where each of the characters, in a complex chain, secretly loves someone who is inaccessible, otherwise engaged or the wrong sex anyway, to *The Echoing Grove*, whose core is Rickie's agonised affair with his sister-in-law, the pattern is, with modifications, repeated. However desirable and however loving the protagonists (and several of them are this) disappointment, failure and betrayal are in-built from the start.

CHAPTER III

The permanent outsider

As a young woman Rosamond Lehmann was beautiful; in middle age she was still highly attractive; even in old age she radiates a physical presence and awareness which has little of the retired *grande dame* about it and more of the woman accustomed to being desired. It is important to state this, because it means that her life experience has been persistently different from that of the woman who has always needed to make friends with a man before she could reasonably hope to attract him as a female. In addition, her personality is warm, generous: women are drawn to her too. With such advantages, one might suppose, life is greatly eased, and many of the problems that attend the plainer, shyer or simply more insignificant woman are removed from the start. Certainly her life history is apparently rich in relationships, lovers, friends and the sort of cosmopolitan social life of which many would dream in vain. And yet her novels present recurrent examples of women feeling unloved, feeling in some way physically or mentally ill-equipped, feeling *lonely* and left out of things. It is, on the face of it, an odd combination.

Her old friend Elizabeth Jenkins remarked to me that she thought that Rosamond's very beauty, and her protected up-bringing, had left her in some ways more vulnerable to uncomprehending hurt than most of us. She had grown no defences in youth – and never grew any. Her very openness to people, her responsiveness that delighted, meant that she never expected pain or disillusionment. I would add that, in addition, I think that she is one of those novelists whose sensibility to other people's realities tends to leave them peculiarly unarmed when those realities reveal themselves as alien and incomprehensible.

It may also be that Rosamond's position in her family, as the second daughter when a son was hoped for, sandwiched between the psychologically more robust Helen and the more distinctively unusual and strong-minded Beatrix, created an insecurity in her at the deepest level. As a background theme, complicity and rivalry, or at any rate tension, between women, is ubiquitous in her novels. It surfaces in the first two via emotion-charged female friendships, then appears more patently as sister-relationships in *Invitation to the Waltz*, *The Weather in the Streets* and *The Ballad and the Source*, and finally becomes a major and agonizing theme in *The Echoing Grove*.

In *Invitation to the Waltz*, both Olivia, aged seventeen, and Kate, aged perhaps nineteen, long in the same way for recognition, excitement, love, but Kate's longings take a more straightforward form and are joyfully gratified – at any rate for the moment – by the attentions of a classic, jolly, wonderful young man, the son of neighbours she has always longed to know better, whereas Olivia's longings seem to be a more fundamental part of her imaginative, vastly responsive nature. At the last minute before the ball, her excitement at the prospect of the dance turns to dread:

Why go? It was unthinkable. Why suffer so much? Wrenched from one's foundations; neglected, ignored, curiously stared at; partnerless, watching Kate moving serenely from partner to partner, pretending not to watch; pretending not to see one's hostess wondering; must she do something about one again? – (but really one couldn't go on and on introducing these people); pretending not to care; slipping off to the ladies' cloakroom, fiddling with unnecessary pins and powder, ears strained for the music to stop; wandering forth again to stand by oneself against the wall, hope struggling with despair beneath a mask of smiling indifference . . . The band strikes up again, the first couple link and glide away. Kate sails past once more . . . Back to the cloakroom, the pins, the cold scrutiny or (worse) the pitying small talk of the attendant maid.

Oh horrible images! Solitude in the midst of crowds! Feast from which, sole non-participator, one would return empty!

She thought of a children's party at the Spencers' years ago; of falling in love at first sight with a most beautiful boy of ten called Archie, a cousin of the house. Dancing the baby polka with him, she had gazed enraptured at his profuse yellow locks and angelic pale blue eyes. Between each dance he took a large broom from the corner of the room where he kept it, and swept the floor. (Why had he done that?) The fourth time she asked him to dance, he replied in a ringing treble, most gaily, most politely, rushing with his broom down the middle of the floor: 'Another? oh, right you are! We've had quite a lot of dances together, haven't we?' And all the grown-ups sitting round the room had burst out laughing; and the sound was like houses falling. That had been the beginning of self-consciousness, of failure of confidence. Some day I'll write a story about it (126–8).

The last sentence distances the reader from the preceding emotion, putting a slight ironic gloss upon it, almost mocking the twentieth-century post-Freudian literary tradition of the sensitive person whose life is blighted in childhood. But there is no mistaking the searing nature of the emotion. When, as a young teenager myself, I first read *Invitation to the Waltz*, I innocently assumed that Rosamond Lehmann must have written it when she was little older than myself; now I know that that novel could *only* have been written by someone for whom the apparently specific emotions involved in it existed in a wider context and thus could not be 'outgrown'. *Invitation to the Waltz*, like its sequel *The Weather in the Streets*, in which many of the same emotions appear in a different guise, was written when Rosamond Lehmann was established in a second marriage with the man for whom she had left her first husband; she was bearing the children for whom she had longed, living in a delightful house with clever and appreciative friends to stay at weekends. But the female creature fearful of 'solitude in the midst of crowds' and of being mysteriously unable to dance to the worldly music others hear, had not expired: she had merely gone into hiding, to surface again and again in the books.

In *Invitation to the Waltz* Olivia's sense of a specifically female inadequacy is substantiated by making her on the plump side and very young: her village-made dress does not fit well, she wonders how many underclothes to wear, takes off 'one layer'(!) but still feels lumpy; her stockings have lisle-thread tops and her nails are unmanicured – 'All those dainty devices, so natural to Kate, seemed when she performed them to become unreal, like a lesson learned by heart, but not properly understood' (126). (The ten years older Olivia in the sequel has 'fined down' and is allowed to be, at any rate at moments, beautiful: her continuing sense of female failure comes from elsewhere.) In *Dusty Answer*, the first novel, which, for all its insights, is much less carefully constructed than others and more prone to rogue romanticism, Judith is initially presented as shy in black stockings, but rapidly blossoms into someone whose beauty is one of the most salient facts about her. This has annoyed some readers down the years, and indeed I think it is a flaw in the novel, but one must add that Rosamond was only drawing on her own experience, and anyway it would be hard to substantiate Judith's relationship with the Fyfes, and then with the college friend Jennifer, if she is not to be physically lovely. It is clear that physical beauty looms extremely large in the Fyfe scale of values. All four confide in her at one time or another – what Julian, the eldest, refers to as 'the common habit of "telling Judith"'. Roddy, the chief object of her feelings, makes love to her, Julian later wants her to become his mistress; before that Martin had wanted to marry her. In the end they all, and also Jennifer, desert her as their own lives move on – 'None of the children next door had been for her', but this is not so much a subject for bitterness and regret as the working out of the novel's theme: essentially it is a book about growing from childhood into adulthood and the impermanence of the passions raised along the way. Compton Mackenzie, the author of *Sinister Street* (1913), wrote to the author: 'My mantle has now fallen upon you.' He was right, if pompous. So, in essence if not in detail, French readers are right when they consider *Dusty Answer* – absurdly entitled *Poussière* in French – as a British version of Fournier's *Le Grand Meaulnes*. The supposedly 'daring' nature of the sexual and sub-sexual relationships portrayed in *Dusty Answer*, which shocked some readers in 1927, are perceived more accurately today as being (like those in Fournier's book) almost pre-adolescent in their unfocussed, androgynous quality. Right at the end Judith reflects that 'She was a person whose whole past made one great circle, completed now and ready to be discarded . . . Soon she must begin to think: What next?' (303) The answer, though Rosamond Lehmann doesn't give it, is surely 'adult life'.

Thus, although Judith's rôle as an outsider is in a way essential to the book's theme, and though she suffers painfully both when Roddy rejects her and when Jennifer abandons her for another schoolgirl crush, she is to some extent protected by her own beauty, distinction and general desirability. The rôle of inadequate, despised female is in this book allocated elsewhere. I have found that readers who have read the book in youth remember, long after the over-romanticised Jennifer and the epicene Roddy have faded from their minds, the awful Mabel. It is one of the few really unkind portraits in the whole of Rosamond Lehmann's work (along with the thumbnail sketch of a rival in *The Echoing Grove*: 'Enthusiastic. Not amusing or amused. Enlightened more than intelligent . . . and making heavy weather of it . . . Steel-true wanton, I rather thought. Well-developed figure, trinkets, head scarves, cheekbones, on the grubby side. *New Statesman* girl. Not *nasty*.)' (291).

But then Mabel is an archetype. We are all repelled by Mabels, feminine or masculine. And we are also afraid, at some level, that something of Mabel lurks in ourselves and that we will, willy-nilly, be co-opted to the troglodyte clan and be dismissed as Mabels by other people, by the Jennifers, the Roddys, the more successful sisters, the wonderful young men . . .

She went on downstairs, looked for the fifth time in the box labelled E for letters addressed to herself, knew for the fifth time there could be none, and went on again, wandering among the ground-floor corridors [the place is a Cambridge women's college]; desired in sudden panic to get back to her room and found she had lost her way.

A girl came out of a door carrying a hot water can. She wore a pink flannel dressing-gown.

'Could you tell me,' asked Judith, 'how to get to a corridor called C?'

The girl looked at her closely and then beamed behind her glasses.

'Oh Miss Earle! Of course! We were up together for Scholarship Exams. Come in.'

Judith, helplessly conscious that this unpleasant dream was becoming a definite nightmare, followed her.

'Sit down,' said the girl. 'I'm so glad you came to find me. You remember my name – Mabel Fuller.'

Oh God! The creature thought she had been singled out for the purpose of soliciting friendship . . .

[. . .] Earnestly her eyes beamed and glinted behind their glasses. Presumably she was kind and well-meaning, but her skin was greasy and pink was not her colour; and her lank hair smelt; and when she talked she spat. The colourless face had nothing of youth in it. Perhaps this was what really clever girls looked like (112–3).

Dusty Answer is a beginner's book and one of the signs of this is the inconstant and shifting level of reality at which it is written. And yet this in itself is part of the freshness and integrity of the whole, in that adolescents themselves do not have a fixed view of life, and the imaginative ones at any rate tend to suffer from a kind of anguished double vision.

Rosamond Lehmann, I think, had this and *Dusty Answer* in mind when she wrote rather censoriously, years later: 'Young novelists should remember that they are not likely to write first class works of fiction until after they are grown up: until, that is, they have compounded with their social and spiritual problems sufficiently to have a *view of life*' [Her italics] (*Britain Today*, June 1946).

In *Dusty Answer*, where the view is not constant, evocations of Jennifer hardly seem to come from the same book as those of Mabel:

Jennifer was half asleep with her head upon the window-sill. The bowl of fruit burned in the dimness. How like Jennifer was her room! Yellow painted chairs, a red and blue rug on the hearth, cowslips in coloured bowls and jars, one branch of white lilac in a tall blue vase; the guitar with its many ribbons lying on the table; a silken Italian shawl, embroidered with great rose and blue and yellow flowers flung over the screen: wherever you looked colour leapt up at you; she threw colour about in profuse disorder and left it. Her hat of pale green straw with its little wreath of clover lay on the floor. Nobody else had attractive childish hats like hers. A wide green straw would remind you of Jennifer to the end of your life; and beneath it you would see the full delicious curve of her cheek and chin, her deep-shadowed eyes, her lips that seemed to hold all life in their ardent lines (140).

Jennifer wakes, she and Judith agree that theories of aesthetics are all rubbish, and then sit together listening to the nightingale before bidding each other a demonstrative good-night.

Rosamond wrote this, and other similar passages, wrapped in the kind of innocence and also perhaps non-judgemental tolerance that today has become impossible: questions about how seriously she 'intended' what to a modern reader is the overtly homosexual element in the Judith-Jennifer friendship are therefore to a large extent irrelevant. There is, however, an interesting subliminal literary pattern here. Rosamond

Lehmann has volunteered the information to me that the main 'original' of Jennifer was 'a dazzlingly attractive girl, still one of my closest friends. She was Scottish, and going to be a doctor, but gave it all up to marry and have children.' Yet she said on another occasion, speaking of the character in the book, 'Oh, I should think she became a lesbian after Cambridge, wouldn't you?' Clearly there were elements in the literary character that went beyond any demonstrable original. Attentive readers of the other novels will notice that she seems to bear some relation to Marigold in *Invitation to the Waltz*: there is the same compelling vitality, eccentricity, ingenuousness (real or false), deceptively childlike garments – even the same reddish curls. But in *The Weather in the Streets* Marigold, though still just as attractive and still dressed with little-girl simplicity, carries another message: her freakishness is no longer seen in quite the same light. She inveigles Olivia into a conversation about lesbianism (yes) which, though it has no bearing on anything that later happens in the book, seems to signify a general warning: nothing is quite as it seemed in the past. Later we see Marigold drunk, and it is made clear that she is promiscuous. In the light of this, it is interesting to speculate on how Jennifer might have reappeared had Rosamond Lehmann written a subsequent book using the *Dusty Answer* characters, but she never did so:* her next book staked out a territory so different that it seems wilfully selected to be such.

The mingled acclaim and outcry that followed the publi-

---

*In *The Swan in the Evening* she recounts how, among the hundreds of letters she received following the book's publication, was one from a young Frenchman who 'withdrew to a mountain-top and there typed out a two hundred thousand word sequel to *Dusty Answer*, accompanied by photographs and letters designed to prepare me for our joint future, when he would teach me love' (66). This experience of having her creation hi-jacked by another's imagination can hardly have encouraged Rosamond Lehmann to pursue it!

cation of the 'sensational' first novel made the author self-conscious. As she wrote long after: 'I had written because I had to, and had thought to write a serious novel. Instead [it seemed] I had exposed myself not only as a distorter of the true values of the academic life, but as a sex-maniac' (*The Listener*, 1953). More recently she has said: 'I began to hate my central protagonist – one of my sub-selves, I suppose (to borrow a phrase from Elizabeth Bowen), embarrassingly vulnerable, self-absorbed, glamorised' (*The Author*, 1983). One knows what she means. It is in every sense what one critic called at the time an example of the novel of limited vision. And yet at a key point in the novel this very glamorised, self-absorbed figure of Judith is punctured in no uncertain way: the 'double-vision' of youth to which I refer above made it possible for Rosamond Lehmann to write the hyper-romantic scene in which Roddy makes love to Judith at night by the river (where else?), *and* to write about her consternation and shame two days later when she realises she has misunderstood his intentions: literature contains few such devastating contrasts, the reality-levels of the two scenes are worlds apart, and I am by no means sure that the author did it consciously:

The web had broken. Roddy had shaken himself free and come close at last. The whole of their past lives had led them inevitably to this hour [. . .] (220).
    [. . .] It was a quivering darkness of all the senses, warm, melting, relentless, tender. This stranger was draining her of power; but underneath, the springs of life welled up and up with a new strong beat. He clung to her with all his force and as if he could never let her go. He was a stranger, but she knew him and had known him always [. . .] (221).

Finally 'He muttered a brief "Oh!" beneath his breath, and seized her, clasped her wildly. She could neither move nor breathe; her long hair broke from its last pins and fell down her back, and he lifted her up and carried her beneath the unstirring willow-trees' (222). That, in the conventions of the period, suggested that something more than a warm kiss was taking place, and it was also in the conventions of the period that a girl such as Judith should take such a development as implying commitment. The following evening she writes Roddy an impassioned letter promising 'a lifetime's devotion', ending, 'My darling, I love you!' which she posts at once so that he will get it the next morning, when he is due to go away. All the next day, she imagines him far off, but having received her letter and perhaps in process of writing back to her. To say that she is disconcerted when, out for a nostalgic evening stroll under the lilacs, she encounters him, is a quite inadequate description of her shock.

'I thought you'd gone away.'

'I'm going tomorrow. A girl I know rang up this morning to suggest coming down for the day, so I waited. I've just seen her off.'

A girl he knew . . . Roddy had always had this curious facility in the dealing of verbal wounds.

'I see . . . How nice.'

A face smooth and cold as a stone. Not the faintest expression in it. Had he bidden the girl he knew goodbye with a face like this? No, it had certainly been twinkling and teasing then.

'Well, I must get on.' He looked up the path as if meditating immediate escape; then said, without looking at her, and in a frozen voice: 'I got a letter from you this morning.'

'Oh you did get it?'

There could never have been a more foolish-sounding bleat. In the ensuing silence she added feebly: 'Shall you – answer it – some time?'

'I thought the best thing I could do was leave it unanswered' (225–6).

Revelation and devastation descend. The rest of the conversation can only be horrible, and it is. Roddy, hitherto faintly androgynous, is now archetypal male, withdrawn, uninvolved, making worldly excuses, devaluing previous gestures, intimating that he had thought the events the other night were 'what you wanted: what you were asking for [. . .] I thought you knew pretty well what you were about' (227–8). Judith feels herself an utter failure as a woman – a failure because she has exposed her passion to Roddy and been rejected and because she has not known the rules of the game in the first place. Even Olivia Curtis's worst imaginings never encompassed this. *She* was afraid, at seventeen, that no one would ever love or desire her, whereas Judith, at perhaps twenty-one, has grasped at love and found it other than what she supposed: it is not, after all (as Rosamond Lehmann's lover Cecil Day Lewis was to write years later) 'warm, a meeting place', but a region in which one can find oneself utterly alone: 'the suicide's grave under the nettles'. *Dusty Answer* may, at moments, come perilously close to reading like a Romantic Novel, but its real message is quite other.

Rosamond was considerably embarrassed by the general assumption, made even by those who much admired *Dusty Answer*, that it was her own story and that she might never therefore write another good novel. In *A Note in Music* (1930) she set out to prove them wrong. She succeeded in one respect almost too well and consequently nearly came to grief in the other. *A Note in Music*, though there is much of interest in it, is not a very good novel, and mainly, I think, because its author tried too consciously to exclude from it most of the elements that had made *Dusty Answer* distinctively and transparently her own. In fact, there is, as always, quite a bit of her own life in it – large, disjointed fragments, at any rate – but they are wrenched from context and heavily disguised. Many years later, she was to tell an interviewer (Janet Watts): 'It became a totally forgotten book, it was even forgotten by me,' and added that when she came to re-read it again herself in old age 'It seemed so not-in-the-canon that I could hardly believe I had written it.' Her first act was, logically, to disguise her central female character as someone quite unlike herself; she told Janet Watts: 'I wanted to get away from any sort of

self-identification, and when I began to write about Grace
Fairfax, I couldn't identify her with anyone I knew, and
particularly not with myself – though later I grew fond of her
and felt very sorry for her' (Introduction to *A Note in Music*,
vii-viii).

Here, I think, Rosamond Lehmann is to some extent deceiv-
ing herself. Grace Fairfax, whatever her limitations, is *not*
entirely unlike the Lehmann-woman we meet in the other
books. She seems, in fact, a classic example of one of those
unsatisfactory *alter ego*s writers construct which are themselves, but with the most vital parts missing. Most of her
defining characteristics are negative ones – the things that have
been omitted: she is uncultured, she has had little social
experience and less sexual, she is not creative, she lacks the
will or the ability to change the course of her own life. Yet
she has (inevitably) her creator's sensibility, her interest in
others, her imagination and also her love of beauty. In many
ways she reminds one of the young Olivia of *Invitation to the
Waltz* – an Olivia who has failed to go out into the world and
gain more courage and expertise. Like Olivia she is overweight,
like her she is slightly old-fashioned in her style and her clothes
never seem quite right, like her (though for a more profound
reason) she feels a failure as a woman. Olivia huddles over
the schoolroom fire instead of going for walks, crying luxur-
iantly over David Copperfield or 'reading *East Lynne* and
eating nut-milk chocolate' (215); Grace's idea of a treat is
when the servant 'drew the curtains, heaped the fire, and left
her with a great cup of coffee and a toasted bun, and a new
novel from the library' (7). Either that, or sitting in the cinema
eating chocolates. Grace, in plain words, is greedy and lazy –
but so, in part, is Olivia. (And this remains true of her even
when she is metamorphosed into a thin, heavily-smoking
divorcée: on her first re-meeting with Rollo she reminisces
about ice-cream sundaes!) Grace's idea of a dinner to look

foward to is – incomprehensibly to today's tastes – fish pie and chocolate pudding, and the reader is not *quite* sure whether Rosamond Lehmann herself thought these yearnings deplorable or sympathetic. The uncertainty seems to have been shared by the *Times Literary Supplement* reviewer when the novel first came out, who wrote: 'If Grace Fairfax had not ordered and eaten with positive enjoyment such horrible suppers as fishpie and chocolate shape, her married life would have been happier, her husband thinner, and her own mind less stagnant' (4 September 1930). He/she considered it 'a disappointing second novel'.

Grace, then, is not such a totally alien creature in Lehmann-land as her pronounced difference from the lovely Judith might suggest. She is, to pick up Rosamond Lehmann's own definition, another of her 'sub-selves', in this case a more suppressed and abandoned part of herself. Literally 'abandoned', for whereas Rosamond Lehmann wrote *Dusty Answer* partly as a nostalgic escape from the alien world into which her husband has transported her, *A Note in Music*, written after she herself had escaped from that husband and that world, is something of an implicit self-vindication. She herself had done what Grace, in the book, singularly fails to do: in the end of the novel Grace is abandoned to her fate – fat husband, chocolate pudding, ugly town, empty life – and though her creator does not set out to jeer at her (on the contrary), it is difficult for the reader to feel that Grace has made the right choice, or that she is other than feeble. Grace has her creator's capacity for romantic projection and thus has the chronically lonely, 'outsider' problem of the dreamer/ visionary/writer, but lacks the more positive qualities that tend to go with this make-up. As a result, the reader veers between feeling desperately sorry for her and thinking that it serves her right.

A year or so after coming down from Cambridge Rosamond

married Leslie Runciman, whose sister Marjorie had been a Girton friend. Runciman was, on the face of it, a highly suitable match: he came of a shipping family, had been an Eton scholar and a Cambridge intellectual and, more significantly, was 'the sort of handsome, clever young man my father would want me to marry'. Girls of Rosamond Lehmann's background married all too readily then, for what else could they do? Even her relatively liberal parents did not expect her to use her degree in a career but simply to 'come back and be a daughter at home'. (When she protested that she wanted to be a novelist and how could she achieve this without experience of life, Mrs Lehmann remarked crushingly, if incorrectly, that the Brontës had managed it.) Any dissent caused by the marriage centred round the Lehmann parents' upper-class resentment when the Runcimans refused to make Rosamond a marriage settlement: it does not seem to have occurred to them, any more than it did to their daughter, that the dour, hard-bargaining, temperance-Methodist North Country background which underpinned the Runciman wealth did not provide the sort of atmosphere in which their daughter would feel at home. Nor does it seem to have occurred beforehand to Leslie Runciman or to his bride that his own attitude to matrimony did not bode well. Like several characters in Rosamond Lehmann's early books, Runciman was typical of that post-war generation of clever young men to whom some degree of sexual inversion seems to have presented itself almost as an ideal, something intellectually and aesthetically more 'right' than the traditional heterosexual, philo-progenitive attitude by then associated with the dead Victorian and Edwardian eras. He shrank from the thought of children. When the engagement was announced, he wrote to a Cambridge friend: 'I know it must seem extraordinary to want to spend one's life with a woman, but Ros is much more like a boy than a woman. She has the mind of a man.' As Rosamond herself remarks, it was a misjudgement of staggering proportions! If minds can usefully be categorised as 'masculine' or 'feminine', then hers must be one of the most feminine intellects ever to exert itself, and her whole life, and therefore work, has been rooted in specifically feminine experience.

In the circumstances, it is not surprising that that marriage was a failure from the start, sexually and circumstantially. Rosamond felt very much the influence on Leslie Runciman of her mother-in-law, a dominating personality who 'couldn't imagine that anyone could like sex'. (Regularly, in her subsequent novels, mothers are good, if at times rigid in their views, whereas mothers-in-law are bad, subversive, destructive: the experience of her first marriage seems to have gone deep.)

One must add, though, that Rosamond herself, yearning as she was to be a novelist, was hardly ready for matrimony at that point, and certainly had not worked out what she herself wanted. She wrote in *The Author* (1983):

It was then [in Newcastle-upon-Tyne] that the problems of identity and meaning started to become acute. Outwardly I was an enviable, popular young woman, married into a distinguished (teetotal) family, mistress of a large solid house in a Victorian terrace, and (good heavens!) of a cook and a house-parlour-maid, enthusiastic tennis player, giver of somewhat joyless little dinner parties (no wine, no spirits – it appals me to remember); and no prospect of a pram in the hall.

Like Wordsworth's Ruth, I was sick for home – not for my actual home, but for a different gentler landscape, other modes of thinking, feeling, future-building. I was assailed by blank misgivings. I was a misfit – I wanted to desert.

What she in fact did was write *Dusty Answer*, first in Newcastle, then, as the book gripped her – and, presumably, the act of writing it worked on her own perceptions of herself – she retired to lodgings near the Dorset coast. In the same way, Grace insists on a holiday alone and seeks out lodgings in a romantically unidentified southern rural spot. But the ominous, unbridgeable difference between her and her creator is that Grace goes there to dream, whereas Rosamond went to write and thus, even if unconsciously, pave the way for her emancipation, both emotional and financial, from her unsatisfactory marriage. By the time the book appeared she had left Leslie Runciman for good.

When she came to write *A Note in Music* she was living in the south with Wogan Philipps, her second husband. Little of her actual first marriage appears in the book – Tom, Grace's husband, is a portly, middle-class bore, a shipping office underling who regrets that he 'never went to 'Varsity' and talks too much about being a gentleman: in other words, he is as different as possible from Leslie Runciman. Yet in other respects very many of the ingredients of Rosamond's own life surface in the book, and she admits that when she wrote it she was to some extent consciously 'getting my own back on Newcastle, and that house by the tramlines and that sort of middle-class world'.

Class; again it is all-pervading. In this book more than in any of the others it seems a crucial element in all the characters' relationships. Indeed, it is endemic in the very setting. The northernness and urbanness of the industrial city where it is set is to Rosamond, and hence to Grace (the daughter of a southern country parson) irretrievably 'middle-class' – if not indeed 'common'. The word is not actually used in the book, but, noting the entrenched British upper-class attitude embodied in it – anti-urban, anti-industrial, anti-commercial, the attitude in which the young Lehmanns and their kind unreflectingly grew up – I am reminded of an elderly relative of my own briskly remarking to me: 'Nearly everyone's rather common in the north, my dear.' Rosamond Lehmann herself had married a version of the wonderful-young-man – a 'simulacrum' of one at any rate: Leslie Runciman himself must have been a slightly exotic figure in the family shipping office in Newcastle, even as Hugh in the novel is. But evidently Leslie Runciman, with his divided loyalties, was unable to protect Rosamond from a sense of being exiled from her true home and kind. It is with a ruthless fictional logic that Rosamond gives her projection, Grace, a husband of another kind and class, more in keeping with the setting. The wonderful-young-man rôle goes to Hugh, whom Grace is destined to love romantically and helplessly. Hugh too is an outsider in the world of granite and tramlines, but not a sad outsider like Grace: he is a joyful, impregnable, enviable one, a messenger from another world. Like the Fyfes in *Dusty Answer* or the Spencers or Tony Heriot in *Invitation to the Waltz*, he and his sister appear in Grace's grey life, unconsciously and carelessly transform it internally – and then depart again, leaving all externally as changed and unsatisfactory as before.

The dust jacket of this novel has survived; it is a fine period example of its kind, its characters in jaunty silhouettes, covering a book whose theme must, in most respects, be regarded as 'period' too. The blurb states: 'The town is visited by two very modern young people; Hugh and Clare. They mean no harm, but by merely being their own charming selves they all but destroy the wedded happiness of these poor provincials ...' A low standard of wedded happiness the blurb-writer must have had, one feels, since Grace's marriage is presented from the outset of the book as an unspoken failure, barren in every sense, while the other provincial marriage reviewed, that of Grace's friend Norah, rather resembles entrenched guerilla warfare! One cannot help having a certain sympathy with the parodist who (in *Time and Tide*) wrote: 'The author's theme is the complete physical, mental and moral degradation of middle age in the provinces, contrasted with the bright, brilliant, decadence of quite, utterly, modern, youth straight from the Varsity and London' (22 August 1930).

But 'decadence' (very much a vogue-word of the era, along with 'modern') is wide of the mark. One feels the parodist must have been thinking of *Dusty Answer* – or of what he had read of its reviews. For though Clare might just conceivably be counted as decadent (she has been married, and separated, and doesn't care, and there is a whiff of Marigold Spencer about her, even to her 'reddish silken hair cropped short'), Hugh is decent-young-manhood personified. Although he has been to Cambridge, this seems to be in his case a badge of class rather than intellect. Judging by his reading matter he is almost as non-intellectual as Rollo Spencer (and with a similar taste in *Tristram Shandy*): the only 'intellectual' books on his shelf – which include 'a novel called *Jacob's Room*' – belong to a more cultured friend, the mysterious Oliver, a poet, whose work Hugh 'unfortunately, had never been able to understand' (67). We, and Grace, first encounter Hugh (like Rollo) in hunting pink: he is out in the country – by implication his natural habitat – walking back from a meet. He is given a lift back to the despised town, and Grace, greatly daring for once, invites him in for a cup of tea. Fortunately the competent servant, Annie, rises to the occasion:

Annie came in with the tea-table, opened eyes of astonishment and delight and remarked gently:

   'Would the gentleman care for a boiled egg?'

She had been with a hunting family once, and knew what pink coats meant at tea-time. Mrs Fairfax, poor soul, would never have thought of it (45).

The egg is accepted, just as the lift has been, wanted or unwanted: good manners, careless kindness and a desire not to wound or offend are the mainsprings of Hugh's character. This is more severely tested later that same evening when he has picked up the little prostitute, Pansy, in a dance hall and given her dinner. He realises she expects him to come home with her: different aspects of decent-young-manhood do battle within him; he tentatively proffers money, it is refused –

'Well,' he said finally, rather embarrassed, 'thank you for your company.'

'Thank you for yours,' said she, and walked away.

He went home and was sound asleep five minutes after he got into bed (69).

The remarkable thing about *A Note in Music* is that, in it, people hardly seem to have sexual relations at all. A whole dimension of life, so important in the other novels, is virtually missing. It is as if the reception of her first novel and marriage into the Runciman family had, between them, temporarily frightened Rosamond Lehmann away from that whole area of experience. She did not, however, stay frightened for long.

CHAPTER IV

In a lower key

I have said that, in *A Note in Music*, the dimension of sexual love and desire is oddly absent: perhaps it would be truer to say that it is there but is relegated to a deliberately low place. Whereas, in *Dusty Answer*, it seems present everywhere in a tentative and unidentified way, intruding even into relationships where it might be expected to be taboo, in the second novel it is, as it were, artificially excluded from polite society. It is almost as if Rosamond Lehmann were, belatedly and transiently, embracing the Victorian literary convention that desire is a depraved characteristic, or at any rate a lower-class one. It is this, as much as anything, which makes this novel, alone among her work, seem to belong to an era remote from our own, when people did not just live in a slightly different manner but *were different* in themselves. Conversely, *The Weather in the Streets*, written only a few years later, in spite of trifling differences from the present to do with servants and private incomes, seems as relevant and real today as it did when it first appeared, if not more so. In it, the relationship of love and gratified desire is central: everything else is detail.

In *A Note in Music*, however, the characters exist in a world in which passion, if there at all, is a force for evil. Norah, Grace's sensibly active, tweedy friend, is allowed to have had a desperate, secret, jealous, carnal relationship years before with a man called Jimmy who (perhaps just as well in the circumstances) died in the war. In an agony of love for him, she learnt to accept his promiscuity and even the fact that he himself divorced lust from love. But this effort of feminine imagination and strength is of no use:

[. . .] To her passionate feminine instinct for life he had opposed his masculine indifference; and somehow, in the general destruction of mankind by man, he had disappeared with a smile and a shrug, and defeated her.

And unfortunately, Jimmy being long since dead and herself having for husband Gerald MacKay, this bitterly-won understanding was rather wasted; for she had married a creature of extreme innocence and chastity, quite uninterested, one would almost think unaware of the difficulties of his sex: absolutely no use to growing boys (35).

Norah's two little boys are the centre of her life, and it seems hardly likely that her sexual relationship with her neurotically ungracious husband (a university lecturer, ill at ease with her vaguely 'county' family) is satisfactory. The here-and-now fulfilment of requited love thus lies firmly in the past for her; her hair is going grey and she is busy making the best of things. Meanwhile her husband, infuriated by his wife's well-intentioned bossiness, falls gauchely in love with Hugh's sister Clare, a passion that he cannot possibly hope will be requited. However, a wealth of angry emotion and caring still lies between Norah and Gerald; Norah's situation seems far less desperate than Grace's. Grace once, transiently, felt attracted to her husband Tom: as she tells Hugh, he was slimmer then and a naval officer, and he was good to her when her father was dying. In any case, '"I was so packed full of unspent, undirected emotions when I was young that I'd have married almost anyone"' (247).

But whatever existed between them seems to be dead. It comes as a slight surprise to the reader to realise that they still sleep together at all, and no surprise when Tom, abandoned by Grace to spend his holiday alone, takes up one evening with Pansy, the prostitute. However that does not seem to work well, even on its own level. Clearly, the prevailing anti-sexuality of the novel has affected him too.

Hugh does not desire Pansy (who appears indeed to have

strayed in from a Victorian novel, as her immoral earnings go to support a mentally deficient brother and she is destined to die of tuberculosis). In fact Hugh seems to desire nobody. It is made clear that though he feels some yearning attraction towards the mysterious Oliver and wishes that Oliver would write to him, this emotion does not have a conscious physical dimension: it is hinted that he has at some point rebuffed or ignored Oliver's physical overtures. This dark side of life is the province of the off-stage Oliver's other Cambridge friend, Ralph Seddon, who is dismissed revealingly by Hugh as '"Queer-looking chap. Bit too aesthetic-looking for my taste"' (133). Ralph asks himself, 'Would it be possible to fall in love with a woman? Could one hope to find one who did not prove tiresome sooner or later?' (158). Are there shades here of Leslie Runciman's reflections on matrimony?

Hugh's immunity from base needs is given a benign interpretation:

[. . .] He simply could not help a soft corner for prostitutes, a natural inclination to be sorry for them, to be polite to them. (Gross sentimentalism, Oliver had called it). Perhaps that was partly why he experienced such increasing disinclination for their services. Nowadays, he told himself, reviewing the sexual temperature of the last year or so, one felt fed up with all that sort of thing. Reaction, distaste set in almost as soon as desire. One wanted – oh! longed for something permanent now, something aesthetically, emotionally satisfying . . . Love, in fact (181).

But this is an isolated occasion, and everything else in the novel points to Hugh being chronically uncommitted, to love or anything else. That is a large part of his appeal for the bogged-down Grace. He has been abroad earlier, to those colonies that still promised adventure then to restless young men. He is only in this northern city working in an office out of pure good nature: 'This was no life for him. It would be easy to go if the old man were not such a dear old boy: if his two sons had not been killed, so that there was nobody – as the old man so often tremulously said – but himself to carry on the name and inherit the great arduously-built business' (65). Predictably, he does go; the end of the book finds him on a liner at night, setting off again across the ocean in the best tradition of the romantic hero. He has not seduced Grace, he has not loved her, he has not even seen her more than three or four times: the one role he has played in her life – but we are made to understand it is a crucially important one – is symbolic. He is, in her words

'. . . The person I've been waiting for all my life [. . .] I always felt there must be somebody who was perfectly happy. You're happy, aren't you? You're not afraid of everything: and you'll always be lucky. Good luck's the greatest talent in the world [. . .] As long as I'm alive I shall think of you somewhere in the world, still gay and lucky . . . So you must promise me you'll be so always' (242–3).

Hugh is – as any self-respecting person must be – very slightly affronted at being told he is always happy ('A lot she knew about him', 242). However, he has to agree that, yes, he supposes he is happy, and that he tends to get what he wants. She expands her theme:

'When I first saw you, it flashed on me I'd seen you before. It was in a cinema the first night you arrived. You didn't see me . . . The next time – that time you came to tea – I wondered again. Your face seemed so familiar. But I know now why. Though I'd never seen you before, I recognised you at first sight. You were the person who was going to mean so much to me' (251).

A multiform concept, which illuminates both Grace and her creator. There is a suggestion in it that the future is always there – past, present and future co-existing – which is otherwise absent from the earlier novels but which begins to surface in the pair concerning Olivia Curtis and is more strongly present in *The Echoing Grove*. It also seems to belong in the context of Rosamond Lehmann's much later remark about the wonderful young man she was 'meant' to marry but who undoubtedly died in the war: it is all of a piece with this that, though Hugh is a living man, he is not for Grace; he is essentially impotent to change her life, let alone rescue her; their orbits just brush and then swing apart again. An aborted, missed relationship is thus at the heart of this novel, which is stranger than its dated trappings suggest. And in the context of the actual story this void is logically right: there is a double-emptiness here, which neither Grace nor Hugh are temperamentally equipped to bridge. Very early in the novel, it is made clear that Grace has abdicated from life; she has given up trying, either at love or at keeping up with the fashions – 'She was fairly comfortable, she told herself (putting in the last hairpin) – quite comfortable really, embedded thick and flat now in her life. Nothing mattered, nothing would ever happen for her again' (7). It comes as a shock of realisation to find, some two hundred pages later, that fascinating, active Hugh has in his own way the same disability:

'Goodbye, Hugh,' she said. 'Be happy. You've promised, remember.'
  'Yes.' He grinned.
  'Love someone. Marry her.'
  'Oh, I'll never marry,' he said gaily.
  'No?'
  'Never find anybody to stick me.' (Any woman would find him out in two twos – his nothingness.) 'Not for more than a month or two' (252–3).

It is left ambiguous whether Hugh's own estimation of himself is a true one.

Grace lets Hugh go, and continues her life with Tom – presumably for ever. For all that the book's title (see Chapter IX) suggests impermanence, immutability is the most obvious characteristic of her own existence. Rosamond Lehmann's own life, of course, took a diametrically different path. To say that she ran away with her wonderful young man and married him (a neat reversal of the more usual gulf between fantasy and reality) would be over-simple: the relationship between a writer's life and the stories he or she tells is more complex than that. However, it was Wogan Philipps who came and worked in the real-life office in Newcastle – and stayed in the Runciman household – and with Wogan on hand that she extricated herself from this ill-advised marriage. She herself says 'Hugh had a lot of Wogan in him . . .'

Rosamond has listed one of the tensions of her first marriage as 'no prospect of a pram in the hall': in Grace Fairfax this situation has solidified into a terrible permanency. She has had one still-born child eight years before, and has not apparently attempted another. This is the core and meaning of the terrible vacancy in her life. This disorganised, big-boned woman might have fulfilled herself in motherhood, if in nothing else, but it is not to be (see Chapter 1). When I asked Rosamond about her, she said 'Oh, I should think that Grace and Tom have given up on sex by the time the novel opens.' In fact this cannot be, since, at a late stage in the book Tom, seeing that Grace seems particularly unwell and melancholy, wonders hopefully if she might be pregnant again. One must allow even the unaware Tom to be acquainted with the facts of life, and he certainly would never suspect her of infidelity. But in terms of general reality, if not literal fact, it is undoubtedly true that sex is finished between them. She is his 'cold and barren wife' (20). And indeed the one redeeming element in this sterile situation, the prospect of new life, of an all-transforming baby, is provided not by the ineffective Grace herself but by Annie the servant. It is the final touch of class-consciousness in this novel of an England that has gone, that Annie not only provides Grace with fish pie, chocolate pudding, silent com-passion, and eggs for gentlemen visitors, but is going to provide a baby for the house also! It is she, not Grace, who becomes pregnant, the servant's classic misdemeanour of the period. Of course Tom and Grace, being nothing if not kind, will let her stay and rear her child in their house. The man in question – a commercial traveller, and married – Annie has sent packing.

[. . .] 'I never told him. I didn't want to put him to any inconvenience, or cause any trouble, not if I could manage by myself [. . .] He's only young. And got two children to keep . . .'

'I suppose you loved him.' (Another improper remark, she thought, Annie would consider her thoroughly immoral).

'Well, he was very nice, madam. If he hadn't been I shouldn't have let it happen.' She added delicately: 'Of course it was an oversight that caused this. Somehow, not being as young as I was, I never thought it would occur.'

Annie, with her fund of physical widsom, was not the one, of course, to let her own ripeness wither unplucked: to deny the needs of her body in the pagan amplitude of its middle years. Love was a term foreign to her vocabulary – an emotion not exploited in her world. He was young, he was nice. They had suited each other. Rather than harm him, she had let him go – did not miss him much. It seemed so simple and right: right, too, that this symbol of matronly qualities should be in truth with child. Annie was a triumph for unchastity (261-2).

So unchastity triumphed. Grace was left behind and Rosamond Lehmann achieved her pram in the hall. The phrase is lifted from the famous dictum of Cyril Connolly (long a friend of hers): 'The pram in the hall is the enemy of promise.' In Rosamond's case this pronouncement could not have been less true. The years when she was bearing Wogan's two children (Hugo was born in 1929 and Sally in 1934) were also the years when she was writing her first assured and outstanding novels, *Invitation to the Waltz* and *The Weather in the Streets*. The processes of gestation and childbirth, which seem to switch off other forms of creativity in many women, in her had a galvanising and liberating effect. The early thirties of the century and her own life were, in every sense, one of her most productive periods.

Nevertheless the failure to bear a living child, or at any rate a child that survives to full maturity, is a theme which continued to haunt her work, become a more powerful image rather than otherwise as time went by. It was there from the beginning. In *Dusty Answer* it is present only in a diffused way; Charlie is a young adult when he is killed, but his death is perceived by the old gardener as the death of a child. (' "Pore Master Charlie – pore little chap ... everybody's favourite" ' 46) and by his grandmother too, who dies soon afterwards. ('He had been her favourite, her darling one', 7). Conversely, the only real child in the book, Charlie's by Mariella, has been unwanted at his birth, and seems odd, delicate, perhaps doomed in another way. In addition, a symbolic dead rabbit appears twice in this book with something of dead-puppy, dead-bird, dead-child meaning attached to it. The first time is when Judith and the others are children and one of them has killed it by accident; she is convulsed with tears at the feel of its 'tender, thin body' (25), its poignant paws. Roddy buries it and makes it a tombstone out of an old biscuit tin, and her grief is assuaged. Then, years later, Martin, good, decent Martin who is the least exciting of the four and is trying to marry Judith, shoots a rabbit in front of her, and is horrified at her reaction of tears and pity for it – which are actually to do with her feeling for Roddy as much as for the slaughtered child-substitute. Later again – after she has gone back on her agreement to marry him – Martin is drowned in a yachting accident. Judith learns of this from a newspaper she picks up at random in a south of France hotel, and for a few hours tells no one else. She thinks –

> ... *Then, in a flash, saw the sea try*
> *With savage joy and efforts wild*
> *To smash its rocks with a dead child.**

*From a poem by W. H. Davies.

To smash its rocks with Martin (277).

Then she flung herself upon the bed, weeping for Martin whom she loved: whom she had left crying for her sake; who should have lived to be loved by his children, and honoured and full of years; Martin who was kind when all else was unkind – Martin who had been dead two days, rolling about in the waves; Martin for whom poor Roddy had searched the sea in vain; Martin who had been comely and now was destroyed utterly and made horrible, – sea-water in his mouth and eyes and hair, sea-water swelling his shapely body to a gross lump (278).

With this death Part IV, the penultimate section, ends. Part I has already ended with Charlie's death, Part II with Judith's father's death. Mortality haunts this youthful novel, but it does not have the force that it will have, years later, in the equally death-haunted *The Echoing Grove*. Poor Martin's death seems particularly emblematic, an image rather than a bitterly individual tragedy. It is, however, a potent image, for in it Rosamond Lehmann conflates the dead child, the archetypal handsome young man, and her persistent imagery of water (see Chapter IX).

I have already indicated (Chapter I) the dead-puppy, dead-bird imagery in the story of Grace, whose only child has died at birth. Reinforcing all this, there is another child in *A Note in Music* who seems shadowed by death, the landlady's only son in the farmhouse where Grace makes her retreat, far from Tom, the city and the north. The landlady confides:

[. . .] 'I'd like Frank to see the sea. Perhaps I'll take him this year, with the Band of Hope outing. But I don't know. These sharabongs don't look safe to me . . .'
She stared wistfully. It was plain that the venture was more than she could compass, even in imagination. Yet Frank, he ought to see the sea.
The child was slighter and whiter than many a child of northern slums. The stock was poor, inbred, unproductive.
She said:

'He's hardy, Frank is. The doctor examined 'im at school, and the report said no disease of 'eart or lungs. Only it seems they want to 'ave out something in 'is throat.'

[. . .] Frequently she spoke of her confinement, her one occasion, her own; measuring time by that supreme event, as who should say: before the birth of Christ or after. Remembering the ten days' rest in bed, the baby, the importance, the ministering district nurse, she smiled dreamily, re-living the miracle of the laying down of her burden, the bewilderment both of pain and joy.

'When 'e was born,' she said, 'the cord was twisted three times round 'is little neck. I nearly lorst him.'

And once she murmured: 'Happiest time of my life it was' (196-7).

Only two pages later Tom, the apparently uncaring, jovial Tom, is passing a melancholy holiday alone contemplating his own childlessness. Arranging for a stone to be raised on the grave of his dead mother (Grace's enemy) he reflects that no one will ever write *'beloved father'* on his own memorial:

Somehow he had always seen himself as a family man – slippers warming – children running to meet him – blowing on his watch – pouring his tea – that sort of thing. And none of it had happened or ever would. He had been cheated and would go to his grave childless. It was not fair, of course, to blame Grace: perhaps she had minded in her own peculiar way about the baby; but she had not seen it as he had [. . .] she could not know, he was sure, would never know as he knew what it really meant to look down suddenly at that form without life, and think all at once, with a most unexpected, appalling and unforgettable pang. *My son!* (200–201).

For Tom, then, *this* was 'the person who was going to mean so much to me.'

In this passage and the preceding one it is as if a large theme which will become central in *The Weather in the Streets*, *The Echoing Grove* and, in a rather different way, in *The Ballad and the Source*, is being rehearsed peripherally and incompletely. The potential results of love and desire – the permanent creature of the flesh which can result from the supposedly transient passion of the flesh – is, arguably, Rosamond

Lehmann's major subject. Via 'the detours of art' she came to confront it fully, in her mid-thirties, in *The Weather in the Streets*, a book that deserves a chapter on its own.

CHAPTER V

The Weather in the Streets

When Rosamond Lehmann was writing *Invitation to the Waltz* she did not, she says, consciously envisage its sequel – though 'sequel', with its deadening overtones of *The Forsyte Saga* and Hugh Walpole, is in any case a misleading term for a novel which picks up the same characters at a quite different phase of their lives. Yet most readers agree that *Invitation to the Waltz*, apparently such a simple tale, a 'charming miniature', as it has been called, is nevertheless imbued with a sense of past and future which seems to come from somewhere beyond its highly contained time scale. The author has said*
that only when writing the unobtrusive but key scene, in which Olivia encounters the splendid Rollo Spencer on the terrace at night, did she think:

I see! *this* is what all this is about! I think I realised there was an awful lot more to say about Olivia's life – an awful lot that I didn't yet know, and must wait to find out; and that meeting was unrealised, it was broken off. But I knew that *that* was what I'd got to deal with later.

In fact, had she written this 'unrealised, broken' scene of meeting with the deliberate intention of setting up the subsequent novel, she could hardly have done it more effectively. Olivia is standing outside in the dark, taking a brief respite from the strain of the ball and feeling lonely and ignored. Rollo appears, characteristically giving the dogs a late-night walk: 'Poor chaps [. . .] they've been howling in the gun-room

---

*Quoted in Janet Watts' Introduction to *Invitation to the Waltz*, 1981. See pp. 270 ff. of this novel.

all the evening' (276). He and Olivia chat, with some slight instant rapport beyond social politeness. She asks him the name of the beautiful girl – Nicola – with whom she has seen him dancing; some tension is associated with her for him; he remarks that she is very young and shy, doesn't talk, and '"Oh I don't know, I daresay she's as stupid as an owl"' (275). A few minutes later they are talking about books: he claims to read and re-read only two, *Tom Jones* and *Tristram Shandy*, but takes Olivia off to see his father and look at 'first editions'. Sir John Spencer, closeted in a small study, is also taking a respite from the dance and welcomes them. 'Nobody knew quite what to say, but they all smiled, feeling friendly and vaguely conspiratorial' (279). Olivia reflects: 'How extraordinary to be here with them; from being outcast, flung beyond the furthest rim, to have penetrated suddenly to the innermost core of the house, to be in their home' (280). A prophetic concept.

She and Rollo return to the dance, encountering the drunken Archie – fallen angel, one-time angelic boy-child (see Chapter III) – on the way. Nicola appears on the staircase and gestures to Rollo:

There was less of appeal than of assurance in the deliberate gesture; she knew he would come. He made an eager forward movement, then stopped, looking at Olivia uncertainly, apologetically.

'I'm all right.'

She smiled at him.

'Are you sure?'

He was still charming, solicitous for her.

'Of course I am, go on.' She nodded her head gaily, emphatically, eager for him to go where he wanted to go, where he belonged. 'Good-bye.'

'Good-bye.' He looked down at her with the utmost friendliness, hesitated, added suddenly: 'I'm so glad we met', and went quickly away.

She watched him go across the room. What a dear . . . He was the sort of person everyone would want to call on in emergencies . . .

His shoulders, his step and voice told them he knew what to do. He would cope, without fuss or self-importance. He was resolute. She was filled with affection, with admiration for him. She watched him and Nicola meet at the foot of the stairs and start to talk earnestly, their head close together. They do suit . . . She went away (284–5).

So the almost woman's-magazinish image of Rollo (not an objective one, of course, but Olivia's subjective view – see the end of this chapter) is subtly turned. He is not for her. She goes stoically away. Ten years later in *The Weather in the Streets* the pattern is the same – and yet on the face of it not at all the same. Olivia, slimmer, more sophisticated, though still extremely vulnerable, married, but separated and childless, re-encounters Rollo. He is married – to Nicola – but is also childless. They re-meet on the train when Olivia is travelling down to the country to see her ill father; the Spencers subsequently invite her over to a dinner party. Once again she finds that she has 'penetrated suddenly to the inmost core of the house . . . in their home.' Back in London, she and Rollo fall in love and start an affair, and for a time it seems as if the pattern laid down by the past must be broken and re-made differently. Rollo's marriage to the inadequate Nicola is bringing him little, not companionship, not children, not even sex at that time: the cards all seem to be stacked in Olivia's favour – not that she herself, experiencing a timeless present of love, thinks in these terms. But in truth such relationships are never timeless or out-of-context. It is Lady Spencer, Rollo's formidable mother, one of a stable of formidable Lehmann-mothers, who tells Olivia much later: '"[. . .] I had long expected Rollo would take a mistress [. . .] And after you came to dine with us that night at Meldon, I expected it would be you"' (275).

It is a remark full of dissolved meaning. Although she is no longer the plump, shy girl she once was, and is welcomed affectionately as a dinner guest, Olivia is still subtly an outsider. Not so much in social class of origin (though there is an element of that too) but by being neither single nor properly married, inhabiting a scrappy, semi-bohemian world of part-time, vaguely arty jobs, in a period when the respectable and the disreputable were – at any rate in theory – more sharply defined than they are today. Lady Spencer does not quite say, but might well be thinking, that Olivia is quite suitable for a mistress but would not do as a wife – even if Nicola were not there, which she is. And although one does not suspect Rollo of thinking in these terms, it is indisputable that he never (except for one isolated occasion) appears to contemplate actually abandoning his marriage for Olivia. The resolution, the lack of fuss or self-importance, the basic saneness which charmed Olivia ten years before is there, but it expresses itself as a resolution of another order, as 'an equable, voluptuous, non-moral temperament' (340) which can tolerate a clandestine arrangement without suffering: not for Rollo the grand, self-destructive, anti-social gesture. He will go on being Nicola's husband: it is not 'caddishness' or coldness (as some readers have mistakenly imagined) that cause him to hurt Olivia, but his very mundane qualities of amiability and conscientiousness. It is these, in the end, which will bring about Olivia's defeat: a defeat more subtle than the simple abandonment traditionally considered the appropriate nemesis for the Other Woman.

In 'The Gipsy's Baby' the child Chrissie, who is the archetypal romantic loner trapped in a large family, visits the Landon-Ellison nursery and subsequently tries to make trouble for the glamorous other family she so much envies. Olivia, in re-entering the Spencer's home, has harboured no such desire; as she herself reflects helplessly at a later stage in the book, since childhood she has been 'in love with the whole lot of them' (281). And yet, like Chrissie, her coming spells trouble for them all the same, and eventually for herself too: in the end, after a traumatic interview with Lady Spencer, she is cast out more completely from this magic circle than she would ever have been had she not penetrated it so intimately.

The Outsider theme runs like a thread through the whole book: it is there in the title. Love itself is a condition of being outside normal life, normal considerations, secretly set apart, but even when the novel opens Olivia has made herself something of an outsider in her own family: the awkward one, not happy or settled, no visible husband, so unsatisfactory . . . The ever-present theme of sisterly rivalry surfaces; home on a visit, Olivia gets a low-key amusement out of teasing her sister Kate:

'Still smoking like a chimney?' said Kate, through pins, beginning to cut.

'Rather, more than ever.'

'How many do you get through a day?'

'Donno. It varies. Sometimes I do knock off for day or two – if my morning cough gets too disgusting. Or if I'm short of cash.'

'You simply choke up your inside with those foul fumes. No wonder you haven't any appetite. I believe that's what it is.'

Cigarettes for supper, and a cup of coffee. Surprising how adequately they took the edge off one's hunger . . . how often, by oneself, when one couldn't be bothered to cook anything, or wanted to afford a movie instead . . . Wouldn't Kate scold if she knew . . .

'I suppose so. That, and the booze.'

Above the scissors, Kate stole her a surreptitious glance. Nowadays it was apt to be a tricky business questioning Olivia. She was as touchy as could be. For the most part her immediate reaction was a sort of defiant irony, extremely boring. Anything would set her off, flaunting the no-lady pose, cracking low jokes – really awful ones – and God know I'm no prude about language, not after eight years of Rob: but it does *not* suit females. Or else she'd simply hoot with laughter. Once, twice, dreadfully disconcertingly, she had burst into hysterical tears (35–36).

And yet it is clear to the reader even at this stage that Olivia is still a hoping, travelling creature. She may think explicitly to herself 'My marriage has failed and my life is empty, futile

[. . .] I shall never have a child in the country' (50), but in fact Kate, safely married to a country doctor and the mother of four children, is the one whose story is over and who is, at some level, disappointed, vanquished. Olivia, for all her dissolute airs, still has the eagerness and the essential innocence that she had years before. She is still 'wanting to make something important enough to be forever' (44):

'Rollo, I haven't had a lover. There was nobody I fell in love with, I didn't try experiments: it was never worth it. Not because I'm cold, only because of love – because I believe in it, because I thought I'd wait for it, although they said schoolgirlish, neurotic, unfriendly . . . It was because of you' (142).

You were the person who was going to mean so much to me.

Rollo too seems to have been travelling, unknowingly, to this point; once his mind awakes he is hoping, planning to make Olivia his own almost as soon as they re-meet on the train. They embark on a private voyage of their own:

It was then the time began when there wasn't any time. The journey was in the dark, going on without end or beginning, without landmarks, bearings lost: asleep? . . . waking? . . . Time whirled, throwing up in paradoxical slow motion a sign, a scene, sharp, startling, lingering as a blow over the heart. A look flared, urgently meaning something, stamping itself for ever, ever, ever . . . Gone, flashed away, a face in a train passing, not ever to be recovered . . . A voice calling out by night in a foreign station where the night train draws through, not stopping . . . (144).

Throughout this first phase of their affair, when Olivia and Rollo transcend their separate personalities and difficulties – their separateness – to become every couple in love, the narrative of the book is partly in the continuous present and switches from the third person to the first: Olivia becomes 'I'. Only when the spell is broken, two-thirds of the way through the novel, and a remorseless development intervenes, does she become 'she' again, with a change that is then desolating by contrast with what has gone before, when love was a place of safety and refuge.

Beyond the glass casing I was in, was the weather, were the winter streets in rain, wind, fog, in the fine frosty days and nights, the mild, damp grey ones. Pictures of London winter the other side of the glass – not reaching the body; no wet ankles, muddy stockings, blown hair, cold-aching cheeks, fog-smarting eyes, throat, nose . . . not my usual bus-taking, London winter. It was always indoors or in taxis or in his warm car; it was mostly in the safe dark, or in the half light in the deepest corner of the restaurant, as out of sight as possible. Drawn curtains, shaded lamp, or only the fire . . .

In this time there was no sequence, no development. Each time was new, was different, existing without relation to before and after; all the times were one and the same' (145).

The art of this and similar passages – an art that goes unnoticed by those who dismiss the book as 'romantic', or who criticise the actions of the protagonists as if they were real people – is that, even when celebrating love it shows by implication what an artificial and partial refuge it is. The candlelit restaurant or the firelit bedroom are, indeed, set apart from the rest of life – 'Being in love with Rollo was all-important, the times with him the only reality; yet in another way they had no existence in reality' (161). In reality, the weather in the streets is still there, and Olivia must still spend a good bit of her time in it, and in empty streets at that. Rollo, for his part, has a life of work and obligations elsewhere:

No one must ask questions, no one must find out. It dashed me a bit sometimes, at first, Rollo being so cautious, always in a stew for fear he'd been seen, recognised; always saying safer not, better not go here, do this or that; not ring up too often at the office . . . (159–60).

Sometimes I remember what he said the time I got a glimpse of his engagement book: 'They can all be scrapped.' It wasn't often they were . . . He can't help it . . . (200).

Yet within this context they do achieve, as lovers will, a hallucinatory closeness that, by intensity, almost becomes the real thing. Only their versions of it differ.

'Now I've got you,' he'd say, 'nothing else matters – all the things I *couldn't* see how to cope with.' Always very vague, but I felt he'd been sad or dissatisfied for a long time in his private life and I wanted to comfort him without asking too much . . . (157–8).

Of course I had dreams of being Rollo's wife . . . Sometimes we'd say, 'If we were married,' but in a pretending way, or joking about how it would be . . . He always knowing what he wanted and intended, I suppose; I being content, I suppose, with a kind of permanent dream, keeping it intact from intereference by reality . . . One must face facts . . . I think that's how it was (165–6).

Olivia has managed to compartmentalize her image of Rollo's life with Nicola by consigning Nicola mentally to permanent invalidism – 'A beautiful protected doll in his house, not a wife . . .' (164). Frequently away, staying with her mother (another of those Lehmann enemy mothers-in-law), or consulting some new doctor ('her favourite hobby', according to Rollo, acerbic for once). Rollo's sister Marigold has told Olivia that Nicola

had a miscarriage once, quite an ordinary one, at least two years ago, and instead of going ahead and trying again she's decided she's an invalid – or her mother has. Her mother's a proper sabre-toothed tiger. I bet she's told Rollo Nicola's too delicate to take risks with and he mustn't go to bed with her. She's always lying on sofas and if she's crossed she cries and her mother says her nervous system's ruined (103–4).

Once again, a dead baby, a childless ineffective wife. This time the theme is moving near the heart of the book:

He never spoke of his own feelings about the baby, he never has; just said once, of course it didn't affect a man in the same way . . . I don't think he knows himself how much he minds; it's obvious to me. When I said once how I'd love a child of his . . . I only said it once, never again, it made him worried and depressed. 'Oh darling, it wouldn't do . . .' His children must be legitimate, they must have the orthodox upbringing and inherit . . . (164).

So, for Olivia, quintessential female with the long-term, female programme built into her heart, the passion is end-stopped from the beginning, pre-empted of an essential com-ponent. Nothing is as 'important enough to be forever' as a living child, the future made flesh. But Olivia and Rollo as a pair can only exist in the intensity of the present, unsupported by past or future. A magic afternoon on the Dorset coast is followed by a night in a big, faceless hotel in Bournemouth; another in Salisbury:

Oh, Rollo! Who were we? . . . There wasn't ever another time like that . . . Crazy . . . Footsteps went up and down outside on the pavement all night it seemed; late cars passed and clocks in the town chimed every quarter and the fire was still yearning red over the ceiling when I fell asleep at last (173-4).

After they start going on weekends together it is harder to accept the rest of life: pain begins to impinge. Olivia visits him at home once when Nicola is away: on the next weekend, in Oxfordshire, she begins to weep: 'It all came out in a howling jumble – I couldn't go on like this – I couldn't – I loved him . . . Why should I stand aside, why should I never count? I realised now what his life was. I was outside and had nothing [. . .]' (192). It is on this occasion, or rather the following morning, that she nerves herself to ask him if he does ever sleep with Nicola these days? He says – fatally – no.

It is then that Olivia, who up till now has been sharing a house in a 1930s quasi-respectable way with a female cousin, gets a temporary flat, borrowed from a friend in her own makeshift world. Now, she hopes, Rollo and she will have a place of their own. But it does not quite work out like that.

The thing is really, I don't like living alone. The wind gets up; or else I start wondering what the people were like who lived in the room before me; dead now, and soon I'll be dead and what's it all about? ... I sit in a chair and do nothing or lean against the mantelpiece [. . .] I was alone in that room more than I thought I'd be. It was disappointing. Nicola stayed in London the whole of the time; I hadn't thought of her doing that [. . .] (201).

Further down on the same page come a few lines which, apparently innocuous and unremarkable in context, may be recalled later by the attentive reader as having a terrible import:

He was in such good spirits all that time, so sweet to me, I couldn't bear to let him see I wasn't on form myself. I'd promised I'd never complain or make a scene again; I never have. The Other Woman musn't make too many demands: Rule the first ... Sometimes I thought – I still think – he was loving in a different way during that time ... What was it now? ... More spoiling, more attentive ... As if he was apologising, wanting to make up to me ... I suppose because he wasn't seeing me as often as I'd hoped ... (201).

Time now begins inexorably to move on. Rollo goes away to the United States for two months for his firm; Olivia gets 'flu, and after that abandons the flat and goes to stay in the country with her friend Anna, painter and photographer, a faintly Carrington figure. Rollo eventually returns, and there is a happy encounter in the country where, for once, the two important human elements that make up Olivia's disjointed life meet and fuse. The idyll seems about to continue and, in August, Rollo and Olivia set off for a holiday together in Austria: Nicola, after a brief improvement in spirits, is ill again: 'I wasn't too shattered to hear, she wanted to go down to Cornwall instead of the trip to Ireland they'd tentatively planned. "And I'm dammed if I see why I should go with her," he said. I felt half-thrilled, half-alarmed, hearing him say it' (221).

Alone together in the 'super-romantic, obvious landscape' of the Austrian mountains, their affair reaches its peak: 'It wasn't long. Only ten days all told. It seems much longer – and yet nothing – a pause without even a breath. We never had a quarrel or an argument. More tender, more dreamlike every day, not in the world at all' (223). On the last evening before they are due to drive down to Salzburg and pick up their letters, Rollo, for the first and last time, seems on the point of throwing up his life at home: he resists the idea of going for the letters.

'"Listen," he said, "you can do anything with me. Only say. You choose. You say." Urgent, insisting almost harshly, throwing the onus on me, like in the beginning' (225).

In a burst of atavistic female emotion she thinks 'I've won!' But, like a good wife, she counsels prudence, patience – and in any case she wants her own letters, fearing obscurely that 'some blow was being prepared, had been launched in our world against our unlawful, reprehensible life outside of life . . . Feeling always that Dad might have died, with me lost, ungetatable, condemned forever' (225).

So they get their mail, and among Rollo's is a letter whose contents we do not know at this stage but which draws him back to England. They part lovingly, and she stays on, holidaying now with impoverished friends from the world of Anna, painting and literary endeavour.

The train journey home picks up and converts into reality the journey metaphor used at the beginning of this section in 'the time when there wasn't any time' (144). She – now ominously 'she' again, and on her own – returns to London feeling unwell. She continues to be ill: unforeseen pregnancy has set in. Rollo is away, unreachable. There is no one in whom she feels she wants to confide, least of all her married sister Kate, or even in Etty her *mondaine* cousin:

'. . . Enter into the feminine conspiracy, be received with tact, sympathy, pills and hot-water bottles, we're all in the same boat, all unfortunate women caught out after a little indiscretion. Give up the big stuff. Betray him, yourself, what love conceived . . . I *won't*. I can lie and lie; I can be alone' (239).

An unwanted pregnancy, at that period, was a thing dreaded by women of all social levels, and the means for ending it – now so readily available – were a matter of desperate and amateurish endeavour, at best the address of an 'understanding' practitioner divulged under pledge of absolute secrecy. An abortion, which is what Olivia has (or rather treatment which leads her to miscarry subsequently) was also expensive then in proportion to the risk involved for the practitioner: Olivia has to sell a valuable ring (Rollo's present) in order to pay for it. It was also by tradition near-unmentionable in literature: I have found no other novel of the period which has anything approaching so direct an account as *The Weather in the Streets* of this all-too-common female ordeal. Not that Rosamond Lehmann's description is in the least 'explicit' in the modern usage of the term: it is simply that the whole nature of the predicament – physical distress, mental distress – is exposed with absolute integrity. The journey-image is brutally inverted:

To be alone, sick, in London in this dry, sterile, burnt-out end of summer, was to be abandoned in a pestilence-stricken town; was to live in a third-class waiting room at a disused terminus among stains and smells, odds and ends of refuse and decay. She sank down and existed, without light, in the waste land. Sluggishly, reluctantly, the days ranged themselves one after another into a routine. Morning: wake up heavy from sleep, got up, one must be sick, go back to bed; nibble a biscuit, doze, half-stupefied till midday; force oneself to dress, each item of the toilet laborious, distasteful, the body a hateful burden [. . .] (263).

When it comes to the miscarriage itself, with an ironic rightness that allows the reader to forget the contrivance of plot, Olivia runs into her ex-husband Ivor in the street outside a cinema, as she is making, with intimations of pain, for home. It is this cissified poet, arty semi-failure, sponger, unloved one-time lover whose child there has never been any question of her bearing, who supports her uncomprehendingly through her trauma. No gory detail is entered into, but evidently even what was there was felt by the English publishers of the period to be too much for its readership, for the published version excises something under half a page which survives, however, in the French translation by Jean Talva. I give it here, translated back into English by myself:

Alone. But I must go to the bathroom. I will because I *want* to. Drawn towards her goal, with a sudden access of strength she reached it. I mustn't lock the door . . . suppose I were to die in here . . .
 'Mother . . . Kate! . . . Oh! Kate . . . Rollo . . . Oh don't tell them about this . . . I should have given messages for them to Ivor . . . To tell them that I love them, that I'm sorry . . . I don't want to die. Tell Rollo . . .
 She died, and soon afterwards returned to life again, on the pale blue linoleum floor of the bathroom. How cold it was! And what a smell of oil-cloth . . . She dragged herself out of the room, up the stairs on hands and knees, reached her own room and collapsed onto the bed, her head buried in the sheets, as if in the abandonment of prayer . . . But I mustn't be found like this . . . One last effort heaved her up onto the mattress; at the end of her strength she rolled, rather than moved, between the sheets.

The English version takes up the tale again, with Ivor's return accompanied by an aged and irritable doctor.

It is worth recording, as a vintage example not only of literary prudishness but of crassness also, that the American publishers of the book first suggested hopefully that the whole 'episode' of the pregnancy and termination might be removed

– on the grounds that its inclusion might affect sales on the ladies' lunch club circuit! Of course this harrowing section of the novel is its meaning and core, for in it Olivia is driven, helplessly, to 'betray him, yourself, what love conceived', and the affair is exposed for what it essentially is. Without the abortion the story would be formless, reduced to a long, poignant, inconclusive anecdote.

Most readers of *The Weather in the Streets* who identify with Olivia – and there have been very many, and their identification very passionate – have longed for her to have the courage of her day-dreams and go ahead and bear Rollo's child and thus make their association real forever. Although the images in that 'burnt-out end of summer' are those of sterility it is, after all, a new potential life in every sense that she carries within her. At moments during her sickly pregnancy, she herself seriously envisages having the baby, although such a step would have been far more eccentric and daring then than it would be today: 'I'll take a cottage somewhere near Kate, and have it without any fuss and bring it up with hers. I'll look after it myself, and plant sunflowers and hollyhocks and have a wooden cradle on rockers, and sing it to sleep [. . .]' (244). Such is the rural idyll, 'a child in the country', as opposed to the implicit moral contamination of the town.

Olivia has no conscious intention at this point of giving Rollo up, but – 'he hasn't written, he didn't wait in London for me' (285) – and Lady Spencer's words and manner have shocked her out of her pregnant lethargy. It is after this meeting that she makes up her mind to go to an abortionist ('*All be as before, love*', 324).

Not till later, when it is over, after she and Rollo have re-met and spent a traumatically unsuccessful weekend away together – all is not as before, he seems to have changed, so has she, the weather is dank and wretched, the inn a mistake – does she suddenly guess that there was another element in the situation, to do with Nicola.

'She's going to have a baby?'

He said yes, and then it was said. It had long been a fact. There was no change between the moment before and the moment after saying it. Nothing could have been simpler.

'Who told you?' he said.

'Nobody . . .' Your mother told me as clear as a factory whistle. I didn't listen . . . 'When?'

He gave a kind of stifled groan under his breath – as if saying, must we talk about it? . . .

'Sometime next spring. I'm not quite – April, I suppose.'

Let's see . . . last July then . . . (333).

So already, even before they were in Austria together on that climactic holiday, he had made love to Nicola. It was, in fact, a letter announcing her pregnancy that drew him home. Everything is devalued, most of all Olivia's own aborted effort, now made ironic and inopportune.

This is Olivia's worst moment, but one cannot help sympathising with Rollo too in the mundane, almost laughable complexity of his predicament. When Olivia reproaches him with having lied in leading her to believe he no longer slept with his wife, he tries to explain:

'But it was true [. . .] When I said it, it was true. I don't think I'd have told you a lie about that . . . I was always more or less honest when you asked me things . . . Only how could I come panting up to tell you –' He stopped, struggling painfully. 'I mean, when it stopped being true, I couldn't exactly come posting to tell you . . .'

Instead, at that period, he was merely 'more spoiling, more attentive [. . .] In fact just as husbands are supposed to behave to their wives when they're up to no good on the sly' (340).

Rather interestingly, criticism of Rollo when the novel appeared came mainly from men. I suspect that the faintly glamorous haze through which he is seen, even at the book's bleakest moments - his wonderful-young-man element – antagonises the male reader. It is also undeniable, as one male reader complained to me, that, with his stereotyped upper-class qualities and his lack of originality or intellect, Rollo simply does not justify Olivia's feeling for him by any objective standard. (Another, female reader, remarked more cynically that this was surely the *point* of the book?) And yet the novel can be read as a classic, objective study in the irreconcilability of male and female needs. Olivia, in spite of what sense and intellect tell her, has not been able to help seeing Rollo as a potential husband, part of a life-vision; while Rollo, for all that he does care greatly for her, instinctively sees the whole thing in a much more indeterminate light, more circumstantial, less conceptualised. As Olivia herself reflects, 'It was only that the word love was capable of so many different interpretations [. . .] There'd been no deception: only two people' (344). Another man, not a habituated novel-reader, on whom I tried the book, considered Rollo 'a big upper-class clot' (a version, there is no doubt, of the 'wonderful young man'!) But he also said, apropos of Rollo's behaviour towards Olivia, which to her is such a betrayal: 'He, poor chap, is just mildly desperate, and these precious moments are what makes life worth living. When things go better with his wife that's an unexpected bonus, and life really is worth living.' It is also the case that Rollo himself is of course much less articulate than Olivia, and with no class tradition of emotional expression – rather the reverse.

It is in this light, I suggest, that one should view the final scene of the novel. Their affair is officially over, but Rollo has a car crash (a somewhat hackneyed literary device in a book that is in other respects so stringent) and Olivia visits him. It becomes apparent that the moments which she remembers as full of passionate commitment he recalls, lovingly, but on a quite different plane, as 'good times'. The last sentence of the book, indeed, is his:

'Do you remember our drives in the mountains? . . . And the heavenly places where we stayed? The little inns? Do you remember the queer one under the chestnut trees – with the funny little band? . . . It *was* fun, wasn't it, darling?'

Fun. That inn under the chestnut trees was the moment when, briefly, Rollo seemed to suggest that they should go away together forever. Love betrayed, indeed, even if the word is 'capable of so many different interpretations'. Some readers have regarded the ending of the book as bitter. I would suggest that it is, rather, a neat indication of something that has been a major theme in the course of the story: a problem that exists not just between men and women, with their divergent biological requirements, but also within women themselves. It is a problem which appears to lie with the dead child, at the very heart of Rosamond Lehmann's writing, and for the moment I may summarise it thus: I have said that the child that is the product of sexual love in her books either fails to get itself born or fails to survive. The children that do survive and thrive, like Kate's four 'beautifully spaced' ones in *The Weather in the Streets* or Norah's two boys in *A Note in Music*, seem invariably to be presented as the product of marital relationships that, however generally workable, are lacking in some element of passion or fulfilment. It is as if the very achievement of childbearing has been perceived by Rosamond Lehmann the writer, in spite of her own experience as a woman, as the end of sexuality, almost the end of life itself. Kate

'was the wife of Dr Emery, living an ordinary middle-class family life, valued, successful, fairly contented. One saw her life running, peacefully, unsensationally now on its course, right on to the end: and why did this make one want to cry? Kate isn't wasted. But there should have been something else, I alone know her, some exaggeration . . .' (258).

Still more markedly, in *The Echoing Grove*, Madeleine, the married sister with her three sturdy youngsters, is shown in a marriage to Rickie that is sexually a failure, whatever other needs it may fulfil, whereas Dinah, if she can bring him little else, has brought him sexual love. As if in *consequence* of this Dinah's child, like Olivia's, cannot survive. 'He fathered her breathing children in lawful wedlock, and in the lawless dark another, mine' (35). Later, when Madeleine does achieve a fulfilling love with another man, her eldest son is killed. A remorseless equity, beyond morality, seems to be at work. By rather different plot-mechanisms, in *The Ballad and the Source*, Mrs Jardine is shown to have lost her only child on account of her own marital infidelity, and when that child in turn abandons her own children the youngest of them – Cherry – dies.

It is as if, in order to remain a sexual being in the widest sense – a travelling, hoping, longing being – Lehmann-woman *has* to suffer the ultimate deprivation of no child, even though she is programmed by nature with the sense that the sexual journey ought, logically, to lead to child-bearing. This is the deeper conflict that underlies the more patent between-the-sexes conflict of *The Weather in the Streets*, and it is this that is implicit in its ending. The idyll in the Austrian mountains that should have produced a child (and very nearly did) is perceived by Rollo simply as 'a lovely time'. And yet, in reality as distinct from wish-fulfilment, it was to Olivia as well 'a lovely time' and enjoyed as such: it was part of the journey of exploration that is uncommitted love; such love and freedom are indivisible, and had Olivia gone on and had the baby then her life would have been changed and defined forever. As it is, 'I expect she went on seeing him,' Rosamond Lehmann has said, to me and to others. 'Yes, I'm afraid it all went on and on. It couldn't become a tragedy exactly. And yet it was.'

There remains something overall to be said about Rosamond Lehmann's method in this novel. It is implicit in much of what I have said in the preceding pages, but perhaps now is the time to state it: it concerns what is technically known as the 'limited point of view'. In *The Weather in the Streets* – and also, though to a slightly lesser extent, in all her novels – there is no authorial objectivity. Everything that we hear and know comes to us via the consciousness of Olivia; even the occasional, very brief, apparent excursions into the mind of Kate are such that one may suppose Olivia to be guessing at them and could have voiced them herself. One academic critic of Rosamond Lehmann's work, Wiktoria Dorosz, has written interestingly about this phenomenon; she says that in *The Weather in the Streets*

there is an almost total identification between her perspective as the governing consciousness and as the main character. Her mood always determines the tone of a given passage. It was different in *Invitation to the Waltz*, where Olivia's profound consternation and distress could at times produce comical effects (for example in the scene with George, where Olivia for a long time does not realise that his question 'Were you out today?' referred to hunting). ('Subjective Vision and Human Relationships in the novels of Rosamond Lehmann', *Studia Anglistica Uppsaliensia*, No. 23, 1975).

In other words, Ms Dorosz suggests that in *Invitation to the Waltz* (and the same might be said of *Dusty Answer* and *A Note in Music*) the reader is occasionally invited to be one jump ahead of the central character in perception – to know, at any rate temporarily, things which the character has not yet realised – whereas, in *The Weather in the Streets*, this gap is closed up. Ms Dorosz suggests that this form of narrative is a twentieth-century one, whose prime begetter is Henry James, and here I part company from her; it seems to me that many, even most, novelists in past eras have used this technique of writing from the consciousness of one character, for at least some of a novel: it is after all a natural technique to employ. Indeed one could make out a good case for saying that this, in essence, is what the novel *is* – a shape imposed by a subjective view or views on multiform reality. Moreover, even when a novel includes more than one subjective view, and occasional interventions from an authorial voice as well, it is surprisingly seldom that these different subjectivities are placed in obvious contradiction to one another, and when they are this tends to take the form of a deliberate and unusual literary device.

It is true that, in *The Weather in the Streets*, the one character's consciousness is particularly sustained and consistent: after all, a substantial part of the novel is in the first person. But to say this is to open up a large and probably unanswerable question. I have said that this novel can be read as 'a classic study in the irreconcilability of male and female needs': I have also suggested that there is a deeper conflict of needs exposed in it – one that lies within the woman herself. But whether the author fully perceived either of these elements as she was writing it is an open question. Certainly Olivia does not appear to perceive them. In other words, one can have a novel written strictly according to the 'limited point of view' and yet the reader may glean from that book insights, implications and examples of which the limited point of view is not itself aware. (For a discussion of the conscious use of this device, in *The Ballad and the Source*, see Chapter VIII). To put the matter in simple, concrete terms, did Rosamond Lehmann, when she was writing the book, see into Rollo's mind and understand to some extent his male point of view though not allowing Olivia this? Or is what she offers us on Rollo the piece of external reportage that it seems? I think that the latter is true, and that not for another fifteen odd years did she attempt (in *The Echoing Grove*) the formidable task of showing both the male and female subjective realities in juxta-position.

At all events, what is undoubtedly true is that Rosamond Lehmann has always been at one and the same time interested in, and perplexed by, other people's private realities. A consciousness of these other, encapsulated worlds, brushing up against her central character's world, perceivable yet essentially unknowable, is a constant thread in her books. It is particularly important in the two Olivia books, and in the next chapter I shall examine this aspect of her work.

CHAPTER VI

Other people

Rosamond Lehmann published *The Weather in the Streets*, that quintessential study of unmarried womanhood, when she was married to Wogan Philipps and was the mother of two children. He had abandoned his City job in shipping to live in the country and paint. In reality the apparently happy façade of the marriage concealed considerable tensions, and was to crack apart by the end of the decade, when Wogan went off to the Spanish Civil War and the arms of a more politically conscious mate. Speculation as to what 'went wrong' with this marriage would be inappropriate here – in any case both the protagonists are still alive as I write – but it is perhaps appropriate to make the point that the compellingly attractive male who is not a husband (or at any rate not a satisfactory one) seems to have been as characteristic of Rosamond Lehmann's life as of her novels. She does not depict good husbands in her books; Tom, in *A Note in Music*, and Harry in *The Ballad and the Source*, are travesties of the genre, despised victims. She singularly fails to depict any lasting marriage – except between persons of an older, Victorian generation – that is not wracked with difficulties and pains, apparently from its inception. The long-term satisfactions, and long-term griefs and strains, of matrimony, do not appear to lie within her territory, and although she has said that she would 'rather have had a happy marriage' than been a successful writer, one cannot help feeling that such a marriage was not written into her personal text.

The interrelation of life and novels is a two-way thing: novelists write about life as they experience it and *also* tend to live their lives according to the kind of books they write. To a greater extent than most people, they do not simply encounter others but cast those others in rôles they have 'written' for them. Thus, when Rosamond Lehmann says that Hugh, in *A Note in Music* 'had a good deal of Wogan in him', one can see that this is probably true – but it is surely true also that Wogan Philipps, appearing at that time, filled with fatal neatness a slot in her mental gallery that was already waiting for him.

To the objective reader Hugh, with his upper-class background, his vitality, his social ease and charisma, his kindness that borders fatally on weakness, his lack of intellectualism, seems essentially the same kind of person as Rollo Spencer. But Rosamond Lehmann has always been adamant that the original of Rollo, and also of Rickie in *The Echoing Grove*, was not Wogan but someone quite other. What this surely indicates is that the basic person, the concentrated image, was there for her from the beginning,* and that at various times different real life men inhabited this image for her, each fleshing it out in his own way. The traditional concept of a fictional character's original is itself, then, a misleading one: paradoxically the original may lie in the writer's subconscious and the real life person may be, unwittingly, an impersonator.

It is clear that, whatever else was going on in Rosamond's life by the mid-Thirties, her sheer circumstances were so very different from those in which she places Olivia that any attempt to find a direct real life correlative to Olivia's affair with Rollo is simplistic to the point of obtuseness. Yet legions of people have tried to do so, including some who (one would have thought) would have been sophisticated enough to know

---

*Or at any rate from childhood. It is no doubt significant that Rosamond Lehmann's primary hero ('more important to me than any other character in fiction', she told me) was Steerforth, the fatally lovable betrayer in *David Copperfield*.

better. The late Cyril Connolly, intrigued by Rollo, apparently nagged at Rosamond 'Was it so-and-so? Well, who was it then?' The answer is that by that time a different man from Wogan had inherited the image of essential young manhood, a real man, who was in love with Rosamond Lehmann – but he was not a lover. He apparently recognised elements of himself in Rollo, saying – one can hear him, in Rollo's voice! – 'Oh darling, that's surely meant to be me?' Rosamond Lehmann has said: 'No one has ever guessed who he was . . . He's dead now. He belonged to a very uncomtemporary world that has gone now. He became for me, almost an archetype; and he haunted most of my subsequent work' (quoted by Janet Watts). To me she has also remarked: 'The lineaments of *un*satisfied desire are very useful to a novelist . . . What in life remains only potential is often the most potent element in fiction, rather than what actually happens.'

One might tentatively add that, in the relationship which is only potential, one is intrigued by what one doesn't know and what intimacy never leads one to discover: however friendly and forthcoming the other person, their alienness remains inviolate. I have said that, in more general terms also, the alienness of other people's lives has been a significant element in Rosamond Lehmann's fiction. It appears centrally in *A Note in Music*, where Hugh, and even more his sister, remain elusive and fascinating strangers to the last: it is also central in a different way in *Dusty Answer*. Although Judith's relationship with the Fyfes and with Jennifer is much closer, much more realised than that of Grace (or Pansy, or Gerald) with their objects of interest, it is still filled with speculation and uncertainty: Judith is presented as having been from childhood a great speculator about other people –

You dared not take your eyes off a stranger's face for fear of missing a change in it.

'My dear! How your funny little girl stares. She makes me quite uncomfortable' (8).

– and yet, at the last, Judith is alone in a Cambridge tea-shop and realises that, one by one, those people whose separate realities she has tried so hard to penetrate and share have all eluded her. Indeed the theme of others' impenetrability might be considered the overall theme of this novel – a theme beyond love, which is just the most intense function of it. It stretches right through *Dusty Answer*, from a stranger glimpsed in the skating scene near the beginning in which Judith is perhaps fifteen – 'This was, to her regret, the only time she saw this handsome and friendly young man, whose wife she would have been pleased to be' (28) – to the point near the end at which she realises that Roddy, the chief object of her obsession with the children next door 'had not once, for a single hour, become part of her real life. He had been a recurring dream, a figure seen always with abnormal clarity and complete distortion' (301).

In *Invitation to the Waltz* the sense of the juxtaposed separateness of other people's lives and views is used almost schematically, with the ball as a natural framework for such kaleidoscopic encounters. There are the polite young men who make conversation about the band or about hunting – confusingly, as it happens! – but more disconcerting, and providing more grist for Olivia's questing awareness, is the so-called poet Peter Jenkin. This is one of the intensely funny passages, verging on caricature, where the reader's view parts company with Olivia's; we can see from the start, what she only gradually and confusedly perceives, that Peter Jenkin is a neurotic *poseur*. When he talks angrily of his parents she is shocked and sympathetic; when he offers to send her a copy of a magazine in which one of his poems has appeared she is flattered – 'How very exciting . . . New Worlds opening. He must be simply terrifically clever. And I haven't disgraced myself at all. He must quite like me, to think me worthy of a copy' (194). Only as he talks on, being extravagantly rude about the Spencers and then about her, does her instinctive attempt to empathize with him begin to falter. 'She began to bleed secretly in her self-esteem [. . .] How incessantly one had to be on one's guard with clever people; what bad taste one could show without knowing it' (200–201).

It is a relief later, at supper, when the dreary young man she and Kate have brought with them to the ball (not a romantic figure, not a wonderful young man but the humourless, priggish antithesis of him) dismisses Jenkin, whom he knows at Oxford, as 'a me-ar mass of affectation' (213). Around her other voices join in – '"Distinctly unappetising specimen" [. . .] "decadent" [. . .] "Give me the common or garden ones who aren't above indulging in a bath and a hair-cut when they need it"' (213). But, though comforted, she is worried because she feels that this is wrong – that she is really on the side of people like Peter Jenkin, not theirs.

He was an outcast, made for hatred and derision. But – what was it then that made one feel that, with just a few more clues provided, one could get to know him, understand his language? I should soon feel at ease with a person like him; receive his confidence. Be sorry for him. Not think him absurd and contemptible at all. There must be something shady in me too, then, something decadent. I'm different from them, though they don't know it. She felt the cleavage, deep, uneasy. I'm not going to do the things they'll do (213–4).

The shadow of the future. And, in fact, in *The Weather in the Streets*, Peter Jenkin appears momentarily at a bohemian party – a part of Olivia's London world separate from Rollo:

Peter Jenkin turned up, of course, he's a hardy perennial, under a pile of sub-revellers, teeny actors and things, he didn't see me or wouldn't – more green-faced, wizened and spiteful than ever. To think of Oxford and the way he poisoned my first year – that note I got: 'It's a pity you didn't see fit to save me, goodbye', in a shaky hand – and when I rushed round trembling faint to his rooms a cocktail party was in full swing, and him drunk and perky, calling out, 'Sorry you've been troubled, dearie . . .' (180).

Olivia's ex-husband Ivor, though not malevolent, seems to have been something of a *poseur* and failed poet too; nevertheless Olivia's original premonition was right: by the period of the second novel she has got a circle of friends who 'do things' . . .

I found Jocelyn, he's only just turned up from writing late, we sat in a corner on top of a table and had a quiet talk. He made a cool island in the room. He wrote down his address in the Tyrol for me, he was just off for six months to write his book; he said why didn't I come out and join him and do some writing too. He always thinks I could write, since those sketches I showed him. He said too I could have his room to work in after he'd gone, he wasn't letting it, he'd post me the keys . . . Dear Jocelyn, you're my friend, you make me sit quiet and consider ideas – that injustice matters and unemployment, and the power and hypocrisy of rulers, and resolutions, and Beethoven and Shakespeare and what poets think and write . . . Things like that, not individual relationships and other people's copulations and clothes and motor-cars and things (182).

Etty, the ostensibly 'glamorous' and 'sophisticated' girl cousin, in fact a pin-brained vehicle for the styles and speech of the era, first appears at the ball too. (Later, in *The Weather in the Streets*, Olivia will share a small London house with her.) She introduces Olivia to a vaguely unpleasant and patronising escort of her own, one Podge, and subsequently says brightly:

'Tell me, how did you get on with my old Podge? He's rather a lamb, isn't he? And dances so divinely' [Olivia has found his gait 'full of breaks and hesitations, quite impossible to follow' (217)]. 'Hasn't he got an attractive *mind*? Sort of whimsical and subtle.'
The dream was beginning to deepen. One could only agree and smile, eager, dissembling (*Invitation to the Waltz*, 225).

Again, in *The Weather in the Streets*, Podge reappears, at

least as a walk-on, the morning after Olivia and Rollo have spent their night at the big hotel in Bournemouth.

'Did you run into anyone?' I said when we were in the car.

'Faith an' I did,' he said. 'A big stiff called Podge Hayward I was at Sandhurst with. He appeared in the lounge with a very hot bit indeed – a redhead. Something told me he didn't want to be publicly acclaimed any more than I did, so we passed each other discreetly by . . .' [. . .] I couldn't bear Rollo saying that. It turned love, passion to derision and lust and squalor [. . .] so after about an hour of moroseness which he didn't notice, I told him the trouble, and he was astonished, but he made it all right, and we came cheerfully to Weymouth (172).

One can't help feeling that Rosamond Lehmann must have enjoyed herself, with the later book, ingeniously slotting odd characters in from the earlier one in a way that would be meaningful and illuminating. For instance the blind man, Timmy, with whom Olivia dances at the ball, and who is there to exemplify the destruction of the war and to set Olivia's responsive imagination going by his own isolation ('a remote figure alone in a far place' – 247) is referred to again in *The Weather in the Streets*: in both books he seems to be yearning helplessly after Marigold, who does not really care for any-one.* The theme of unreciprocated love haunts Rosamond Lehmann's work. Still more plausibly we find it exemplified, in the second Olivia novel, in George. In the first one, he was the splendid young man who inadvertently made her feel inferior because she did not understand about hunting; in the second, seen now through adult and more experienced eyes, he is just obliging and commonplace – and vulnerable himself:

'He looked lonely all by himself, receding at the other end of the enormous room, his simple round oil-sleeked head gleaming, his stiff shirt stark and bleak, his neat shoulders rigid above the table,

*During the war Abney, the original of the 'house next door', became a weekend convalescent home for blinded officers.

patiently squirting a syphon – expecting nothing after all these years
of being in love with Marigold; waiting for nothing but his drink'
(122).

(It is, incidentally, George whom Rollo uses as his alibi
when he wants to spend time with Olivia.)

The relative decline in the happiness and successfulness of
both Timmy and George from the one novel to the other (and
indeed of Etty and Podge and Peter Jenkin and Marigold
Spencer too) is a significant, though understated, theme in *The
Weather in the Streets*. It is a social theme, to do with the First
World War and the period leading to the next one, which was
to be brought out more strongly in *The Echoing Grove* (see
Chapter VII). In the Olivia books it is particularly exemplified
in Archie, who is one of Olivia's many painful and illuminating
experiences at the ball: she tries to talk to him, not understanding that he is drunk. He crops up ten years later in a convincingly sinister light; he is referred to uneasily at the initial
Spencer dinner party – clearly his degenerate ways have become an open family problem. Then, much later in the book,
when Olivia and Rollo are having their agonised truth-telling
session – Olivia has told him about her abortion, he has
admitted Nicola's pregnancy – Archie slots in again:

[. . .] 'When we were married,' he said with a great effort, 'she wasn't
in love with me. I knew it. She'd always been in love with another
chap.'
    'Archie?'
    'Yes, Archie . . . how did you know? . . . He went all out after her
and then . . . he sort of backed out. It's a favourite little trick of his
[. . .] She had the hell of a time . . . She takes things terribly to heart
. . . and she can't sort of express herself . . . She agreed to marry me
on the understanding – I'd sort of be there – you know – she could
rely on me . . . As long as she wanted me about I wouldn't snap out
of it. It worked fairly well for a bit . . . and then – ' He stopped,
swallowed. 'Then there was this baby business. It sort of upset her,

you know. Everything seemed a failure all round ... she got into a sort of state – '

'Poor girl ...' Yes, I see ... Now one must accept her as real, as human and suffering (341).

Nicola, indeed, is the archetypal Other Person, the mysterious stranger whose existence and reality matters so terribly to Olivia but who, in effect, can never have any reality for her. The 'one must accept her as real' is theoretical, not felt. She remains to the end of the novel the statuesque vision glimpsed ten years before on the staircase at Meldon, or the doll-like invalid in the soft bed.

Other strangers, less closely integrated into the web of the two novels but nevertheless important to their texture, crop up in both books. The cheerful, Girl Guiding Martin girls, who appear at the ball – 'Good old Martins. When all else was lost their presence could always be counted on at the buffet' (180) – are mentioned in the later book, partly as an incidental device for setting the tone of conversation between Mrs Curtis and her daughters, the sort of humorous study in imperfect, defensive but feeling-laden communication at which Rosamond Lehmann excels. Dolly Martin is going to be married (like plain Mildred in 'The Red-haired Miss Daintreys') to a man whose work lies in China:

'She'll be captured by bandits,' said Olivia, 'for a cert. She's got just the looks they always pick on. A few more years shall roll and Dolly'll be held for ransom in a bandit lair. I see her photo in the papers now.'

'These missions do wonderful work,' said Mrs Curtis with a touch of severity: for why should everything be made a mock of? 'It's a hard life and a dangerous one.'

'Serve 'em jolly well right for interfering,' said Olivia harshly.

'People must do something, I suppose,' Kate yawned.

'His name is Potts,' said Mrs Curtis, passing on with determination to the particular. 'Cyril Potts, – or was it Cecil? Not a very romantic name,' she conceded, smiling; for of course they thought it funny –

'But Dr Martin says he's got such a particularly nice open face. Olivia, you might send her a line, I thought. She was always more your friend.'

'I might.'

'I've been wondering what I could give her that would be really useful.'

'A cake-basket.'

'A cruet-stand . . . or two cruet-stands.'

'I thought perhaps a little cheque, really, then you girls could give her a little something personal. From the two of you. You needn't spend much.'

'No, we needn't,' said Kate. 'It's the thought that counts.'

'Poor Dr Martin, I'm afraid he'll miss her dreadfully. But Phyl's coming home to keep house for him. You know she's been sharing a cottage in Wiltshire with a friend, a Miss Trotter, and breeding – now, what is it? – Angoras, I think.'

'Poor old Phyl,' said Olivia. 'It's a shame she should have to give up her career. Hard on Miss Trotter, too. You don't find a pal like Phyl on every blackberry bush.'

'Yes, Dr Martin was a little unhappy about it, but she would. She never hesitated. Those girls have always been so devoted to their father.'

'And she may be able to do something with rabbits here.'

Oh, give it up! . . . Plain, cheerful Martins, companions of childhood, coping efficiently with their lives, sensible women . . . Dolly would never wake up one morning in China and tell herself: My marriage has failed and my life is empty, futile. Not she. Dolly scored heavily (58-9).

. . . 'Has anyone taken Mrs Skinner's cottage yet?'

And after that I'll ask for details of Miss Robinson's complete breakdown . . . And after that . . .

Across the table they began to ply a peaceful shuttle between the three of them, renewing, re-enforcing, patching over rents and frayed places with old serviceable thread. They were tough still; they were a family. That which had chanced to tie them all up together from the start persisted irrevocably, far below consciousness, far beyond the divergences of the present, uniting them in a mysterious reality, independent of reason. As it was in the beginning, is now . . . (59–60).

Major Skinner, a well-intentioned, disreputable old person who wanted to teach Olivia to play golf, was one of the numerous people whose own version of reality she found it hard to repudiate when she was seventeen. He is now dead. Miss Robinson was the dressmaker who, in *Invitation to the Waltz*, made Olivia's flame-coloured dress for the ball, rather badly. Hints, in that book, of her frustration and hysteria, are cleverly expanded, in the later book, into something more patent, symbolic of the female plight in general and perhaps of the gathering sense of social decline and doom already mentioned above. All is not entirely as it was, is now . . .

Not dangerous at all: only very trying turns. She wouldn't do her hair or bother to dress. Go out, even for a second into the back garden, she would not; and write anonymous letters she occasionally did; only the post office Miss Robinson was generally able to intercept them; not obscene, but calvanistic, minatory, or in the style of warnings – straight tips from God's confidential agent; certain damnation pronounced on Winnie Pratt, the stationmaster's daughter, fornicatress; a message from the Lord to the young milkman; a hint, no more, to the vicar about Miss Sibley, his housekeeper, instrument of Satan . . . Also they'd had to lock up the piano with its rose-silk fluted bodice, she made such a din on it in the middle of the night, at dawn – waking the neighbours. She'd cried bitterly at that – oh! how she'd cried. They'd thought of doing away altogether with the piano to spare her feelings, only it had always been there like in Dad's time and his father's before him: the place would seem funny without it . . . (129).

The stylised echoes of uneducated voices in this passage tend to conceal a more serious theme in it: messages may, with poor Miss Robinson, be a form of madness, but the sense of some less specific but important message frequently accompanies the appearance of a stranger in Rosamond Lehmann's work. Much later in the same novel, when Olivia is isolated in London, 'alone, sick [. . .] in this dry, sterile, burnt out end of summer' in 'a third-class waiting room at a disused terminus' (263) rather than on the exploratory journey of love, she encounters people in the park who give her the sense of communication from other worlds, other realities, potent yet ultimately unanswerable. One day it is a middle-aged man in a grey serge suit, who talks to her about cars, and his nerves, and urges her to accept a pen-knife with a religious text engraved on it. Another day it is a woman with a 'composed, pleasant, superior parlour-maidish voice' accompanied by a very small boy who is mysteriously unwell – ' "Fits. Yes. Two a week he gets . . . Only a miracle can save him, the doctors say" ' (268). Again, the dead or doomed child, a bad omen for Olivia, who is carrying the potential child she is soon to have destroyed. Another time it is a young man, and this is a slightly strange passage in itself, for it seems to suggest a previous acquaintance between him and Olivia – or perhaps he simply stands for a number of his kind:

A trial to friends, an anxiety to parents. He talked too much, he trusted everybody, incurably expecting from human nature some behaviour that would not occur; crying then, 'Traitor! Swine!'; next turning cynic, thanking God with mirthless barks of laughter for a sense of humour [. . .] When winter came he caught a bad cold. He drank the smutty milk out of the bottle on the doorstep and turned his face to the wall. When it was night he felt lonely. He got up, and having no dressing-gown wrapped himself in the plush tablecloth and looked out of the window at the lights of London. He thought about being unloved and about the sufferings of humanity, and wept. She bought him a muffler. 'You must wrap up.' So he did. He wore it always, right through the summer. She befriended him and he liked her, but soon he passed on, away from her: she was not what he sought. Nobody would be that. There was no comfort in him. He was of the breed of Jocelyn; of that one who came one night to Jocelyn's door. James was turning into something like that, walking through France, secretively filling up his copybook . . . There seemed to be a good many of them striding about Europe, looking thin. Not safe, conformist young men. Perhaps more important [. . .] than Rollo (269–70).

James, the little boy who, in *Invitation to the Waltz*, makes up poetry (some of it originally made up by John Lehmann) and who proudly gives Olivia a hideous vase for her seventeenth birthday, has turned into one of these formidable, haunting strangers. Early in *The Weather in the Streets* he appears, in long-range, as an unhappy adolescent whom the family are trying to edge into the family business, his room 'so burdened with him, stricken, sensual, poignant with his penned-up mysterious youth, his harsh male unhappiness; the tidiness of concealment everywhere . . .' (39). Towards the end of the book he has managed to escape into adulthood and turns up, 'a large young man in a dark suit that needed pressing' at one of the heterogeneous parties Olivia frequents: 'He looked at her under his eyelids. She noticed that he had that look of a bird of prey . . . a wild or untamed version of Dad's and Uncle Oswald's look of a queer bird. A notable young man, alarming' (356).

Uncle Oswald is another potential messenger, a seedy, faintly sinister but basically kindly visitor in the Curtis household, subject – in the earlier book – of uncertain interest to the two girls:

'I wonder what he does in London?'
'I believe he's a sort of librarian or secretary to someone – now and then.'
'It must be very now and then. He's nearly always here. And I'm sure Mother doesn't like having him. It's queer. I asked Dad once if it was true he was awfully brainy: because I'd heard somebody say so: Aunt Edith I think. And Dad said: He was once; but after he left school he never had very good health. Dad sounded awfully sorry somehow. I didn't like to ask any more [. . .]' (30).

Mr Curtis himself has something very slightly mysterious about him, at odds with his indefatigably sane wife, a hint of other worlds, other possibilities never realised, or abandoned:

He had come to fetch them once from a party dressed in a black mackintosh cape and the most shaming German hat with a little feather in it. He played the flute. As a boy, he had spent summer holidays walking through France and Germany playing for his bread and butter, sleeping on haystacks, under hedges. He walked through legendary villages at evening, playing on his flute, and all the people came running and tumbling out of their houses and danced after him. That couldn't be true really: the clothes, the setting belong to the Pied Piper. All the same she saw him clearly, indestructibly: his shock of hair, his shabby eccentric coat, his face of a queer bird, melancholy, heavy-lidded [. . .] How did it all fit in with having to go to the mill with Grandfather and learning to be a business man? (15–16).

Ten years later, at the opening of *The Weather in the Streets*, he is very ill with pneumonia. Afterwards, although technically recovered, he is no longer the man he was, a figure in a wheeled chair:

There he lay. Sometimes he knew one, sometimes he didn't [. . .] After all he hadn't said – whatever it was he should have said, had been on the point of saying. He'd given up, let it slip; and now it didn't matter [. . .] Almost she leaned forward to say: 'Dad, are you pretending?' – the notion was suddenly so strong that he was still there, that it was all assumed, out of perversity, laziness, disillusion-ment: as people decide to be deaf. But the moment passed. He was far out of earshot (251–2).

It is because her father has pneumonia that Olivia comes home to visit, and this is how she re-meets Rollo on the train. The coincidence of events is, in thematic terms, no coincidence: the conjunction of sick father versus lover is one that repeats itself many times in Rosamond Lehmann's work. It is almost as if the disablement or death of the father is the price the characters have to pay for the freedom to give their love elsewhere. Coming back into her childhood home, having been sitting for some time with Rollo in the dark car, Olivia goes to her sick father's room to see how he is. This is the occasion on which he seems to be 'on the point of saying' something. He tells her, apparently at random, '"No need to go on regretting . . . suffering for things. Morbid. Remorse's a nasty habit. Bad Pol'cy. All make mistakes. You've got'r life b'fore you"' (138). She kisses his forehead, thinking 'What a different kind of kiss' (139), and reflects that he speaks 'in a blurred way – rather like the other, like Rollo's father' (138). For it is not only women characters in Rosamond Lehmann's work for whom this father-lover tie is true. Rollo's father also has been seriously ill and, as Mr Curtis will be, is now 'recovered' but forever impaired. Olivia has encountered him at the dinner party, being gently eased along by his wife, losing track of conversations. She reflects: 'What about the women in *his* life? He must have been a handsome man, virile, well set-up, like Rollo. What memories were shut inside his head, or what had he forgotten? *Dear dead women with such hair too . . .*' (111).

Similarly, in *Dusty Answer*, Judith's elderly father dies suddenly at the end of Part II, marking a significant phase in the development of her relationship with the Fyfes. In *A Note in Music* it has been the death of Grace Fairfax's father that propelled her into the arms of Tom, who happened to be there and supportive at that particular moment. And eventually, in *The Echoing Grove*, as in *The Weather in the Streets* but more intricately, the illness and death of the father is woven into the plot: it is the father's illness, while on a visit to South Africa, that sends his daughter Madeleine off there and thus enables Rickie and his other daughter, Dinah, to come together again and (like Rollo and Olivia) take a clandestine holiday which very nearly transforms itself into a permanent escape. (It is the *mother's* death, many years later, that finally brings the two estranged sisters together again.)

The source of the ill or dying father in the Lehmann books is not far to seek. Rudolf Lehmann contracted Parkinson's Disease during the First World War, when his daughters were adolescent, and lingered till 1929 in a state of increasing physical and mental decline. This actual situation is allowed to surface fictionally in the book *The Ballad and the Source*, in which Rosamond Lehmann made undisguised use of her own family background (see Chapter 1) and in one of her short stories, 'The Red-haired Miss Daintreys'. In this story the children take a great fancy to a family met on holiday in the Isle of Wight, whose adult daughters, genteel Edwardians, represent to Rosamond-Rebecca a whole various world of Other People. The Daintreys are invited to Bourne End; later the narrator and her family all attend Mildred Daintrey's wedding in London – 'And that was the last time we saw the Daintreys. It was about then that my father embarked uncomplainingly upon the long course of his last illness, and we ceased to invite friends for week-ends' (*The Gipsy's Baby*, 87).

The explanation is factual, but its significance, in the context of the story, is potent: Mildred Daintrey has had a crush on Rebecca's father for some years; he is now in decline, she is married, becomes pregnant. (The pregnancy, however, brings about her own death, and produces no living child. Shortly after this the story ends, with the comment 'the mould is broken that shaped and turned those out [. . .] There will be no more families in England like the Daintrey family' (90). Thus in the brief compass of this story several basic Lehmann-themes appear in a most concentrated inevitable form.)

There is another dying male in *The Weather in the Streets* who seems to have a symbolic function in the story of Rollo and Olivia: Simon, Olivia's artist friend. Anna, the painter and photographer, has cherished a long-term passion for him, and her essentially unrequited love proceeds in counterpoint to Olivia's. Anna is the only person in whom Olivia confides; she is, perhaps, an idealised sister-figure in whom one can trust without the real-life wariness, and there is a notable – and unique – moment when Olivia is staying with Anna, Rollo comes to visit for the day, and is happily absorbed for a few hours into Olivia's other world. This happens at Simon's cottage in the country where Anna is living: later, when the landscape of Rollo and Olivia's affair has changed and darkened, they borrow the cottage themselves, intending to spend the weekend there, but the magic has gone from it: 'It was a small white house with green shutters and a leaded roof, set in a piece of neglected lawn: dismal, unwelcoming. Nothing special about it except the ragged thorn hedge all round. The shrine was broken, the genius had departed' (320). By that time something else has happened besides Olivia's abortion: Simon himself is dying of typhoid in France.

Effective as the symbolism of this is, I feel that the delineation of the Simon-Anna-Jocelyn-Colin group of characters is the only part of *The Weather in the Streets* which is not successful in its own terms. It was obviously necessary – and realistic – that Olivia should be provided with *some* sort of present social context, however sketchy and shifting, but the fact is that those characters, particularly Anna and Simon, are visualised with insufficient detachment: 'limited vision' here transcends its own fictional utility and tips over into the kind of indulgence that is more appropriate to description in a letter than in a novel. It is as if, in these sections, we are hearing Olivia's voice talking not to herself but to some other friend:

Anna does love that house. She says one could paint all one's life within a two-mile radius from the door. Morning, afternoon, evening, she scuttled out with her easel – whenever she wasn't cooking, in fact. She likes cooking, she did more of it than me, I'm afraid. She had depressed times about her painting, and scrapped two-thirds, but she thought she was getting on better on the whole. All the rooms smelt of turpentine and wet canvases. She was preoccupied at meals and forgot to comb her hair, and had streaks of paint on her face. Dear Anna, I do like her so much. She's so quiet . . . (211).

Of this group of people, one critic has written that they 'are supposed to possess qualities (Anna's integrity, Simon's spiritual power) of which we are only told by Olivia but which are shown unconvincingly or not at all: they are more a function of Olivia's interest in them than realised characters' (Wiktoria Dorosz). This seems to me true, but I would suggest a further reason for their relative unconvincingness. I have elsewhere described Anna as something of a Carrington-figure – Dora Carrington, the artist woman-friend of Lytton Strachey – and since Simon dies of typhoid nursed by Anna, and Strachey died (in 1934) of what was believed to be typhoid* nursed by Carrington, it is hard not to assume *some* association between the fictional characters and the real-life ones, who were Rosamond and Wogan Philipps' close friends. Particularly when you know that Carrington placed a crown of evergreens from the garden on the dead Strachey's head, and in *The Weather in the Streets* Anna is made to say apropos of Simon '"After he died [. . .] I made him a wreath of bay. He looked so triumphant"' (377). I am not suggesting that Simon is any kind of portrait of Strachey: clearly he is a different, less abrasive kind of person. I merely note that in relation to *Anna* he seems to play something of the same role as Strachey did to Carrington. After his death someone else says of her '"She's been going through old papers of his all day – burning a lot – and sorting his clothes and things. She wants to distribute them and be done with them. She's quite calm. I don't think she sleeps . . ."' (355). Olivia thinks 'Oh Anna! . . . If she wouldn't look at us as if we were shadows' (354). In the book the suggestion is that Anna survives to re-make her life, but in fact Carrington killed herself seven weeks after Strachey's death.

When I suggested these part 'sources' of the Anna-Simon

---

*Actually a post mortem revealed it to be cancer of the stomach. A Runciman cousin, however, did die of typhoid.

group in the novel to another literary personage whose memory goes back that far, she said that this could hardly be – that Ham Spray, Strachey's house where Rosamond and Wogan were often guests, was altogether grander than the modest cottage depicted in *The Weather in the Streets*. This however seems to me irrelevant. It would also, of course, be true that the real-life Strachey circle was more intellectual, exotic and altogether outstanding than the circles penetrated by Olivia – but this again is irrelevant and indeed inevitable. A writer who becomes famous, as Rosamond Lehmann had by the time *The Weather in the Streets* was written, can hardly endow her characters with *all* the attributes of those who are now her natural companions, any more than she can make her protagonist a faithful representation of herself even to the exceptional success. Thus, just as Olivia possesses all her creator's important characteristics except one – the drive to become an effective writer ('[Jocelyn] always thinks I could write, since those sketches I showed him.' 182) – so the Anna-Simon group exude much of the atmosphere of the Strachey-Carrington circle without having the exceptional attributes which made them what they were.

This, I would suggest, is why there is something fudged about the Anna-Simon element in the novel, something that does not entirely convince the reader he is hearing the truth – not, at any rate, truth at the high standard that prevails for the rest of the book. Paradoxically, in this novel that has caused women to write in numbers to the author to say 'Oh Miss Lehmann – you've written my story!', the only sections of it that do appear to arise identifiably from Rosamond Lehmann's own concurrent circumstances and relationships are the only ones that fail to seem quite real.

Another war

In 1939 Rosamond Lehmann wrote her only play. It was performed that summer in a few Sunday shows with an impressive cast – Jack Hawkins, Margaret Rutherford, Ann Baxter and the author's own sister, Beatrix Lehmann – but nothing further came of it. It was called *No More Music*, a title that seems to relate less to its ostensible plot than to a sense of an epoch ending that pervades it. It takes place on an island in the West Indies, which the author had first visited earlier in the decade, and some of its locational detail was to reappear forty years later in the author's belated novel *A Sea-Grape Tree*. Its central characters are a painter of uncertain temperament and his long-standing, embattled girl friend. It is not – the author would now agree – a satisfactory piece of work, and it is hard to see why Rosamond Lehmann, who is so much mistress of the interior monologue, should have supposed that her talent would adapt well to the theatre. However, popular novels were so regularly dramatised at that period, whether their style was suited to the treatment or not, that no doubt the distinction between a fictional creation and a theatrical one was then less sharply perceived than it is today. *No More Music* is chiefly significant in Rosamond Lehmann's work for its hints of a social crack-up, its setting in an island boarding house populated by people living in blinkered worlds of their own, and its theme of callous male/rejected female. By the following year the Second World War had fully come, and Rosamond Lehmann's second marriage had ended. It is instructive to compare the preoccupations of the play with what the author has herself told an interviewer about this period:

My marriage became pretty stormy. I thought we were going to be happy ever after but unfortunately we weren't. It was a period of anxiety and sadness; and there was a terrible feeling of approaching doom in the 1930s – certainly from the time of the Spanish Civil War which Wogan went out to fight in [. . .] If I looked inside myself I was always rather frightened, thinking: 'This marriage looks as if it's going to collapse.' But outwardly I suppose I was a happy young mother with beautiful children. It was hard to make sense of it all ... I never felt I belonged to any group. I never felt I belonged anywhere. [. . . In 1940] we left the house, and I took the children back to my mother, who wasn't at all pleased to see me. I was desperately bereft and lonely, trying to keep going for the children. Then I became a reader for my brother when he was editing his magazine *New Writing* ...' (Janet Watts, *Harper's & Queen*, November 1982).

John Lehmann's publication was one of the most distinguished to come out of the war years. It had a number of outstanding contributors, and it was for it that Rosamond Lehmann wrote, during the war, her short stories that were subsequently gathered together in the collection that takes its title from the first of them – *The Gipsy's Baby*. The novel she published in 1944, *The Ballad and the Source*, was also begun as a short story, as the reappearance in it of the Landon-Ellison family suggests, but it rapidly evolved into something much bigger. According to Rosamond, 'Mrs Jardine just became *enormous*.' The stories that remained short were the only things she has ever written in her life to order – her brother wanted them from her. With the practical realities of wartime life in the country (she had left Fieldhead again and was living with her children in a cottage elsewhere in Berkshire) – 'it was difficult to fit writing in, but one had so much more energy in the war'.

War, the previous war and the current one, are the dominating presences in this collection, although largely unseen. It is as if the war which had blighted her later childhood and rooted in her creative consciousness the image of the splendid but doomed young men – 'lost boys' and 'dream figures', as she has described them – had simply been biding its time, lurking there continually below the horizon in the 1920s and 1930s, and when it showed its face again in 1939 the sense of disaster was mitigated with a degree of relief. The hidden enemy had returned, and one could face it after all.

None of this is made explicit in the story collection, but the order in which the stories appear (and were written) makes its own point. The first two, the one about the Wyatts (see Chapter 1) and 'The Red-haired Miss Daintreys' are rooted in a lost world. But whereas the Wyatts seem to belong to Edwardian England, pre-First World War, pre-father's illness, the 'Miss Daintreys' spans the moment of change and break-up. The first part of the story takes place in the idyllic setting of the Isle of Wight, where the Lehmann-Ellison family take their summer holidays. It is another of those instances in her work where the place seems to be the starting point for a whole creation, and the passage between the Enchanted Isle and the mainland is intensely evoked:

Now comes the best of the voyage, when the boat leaves the channel and begins to wind through ribbony deep-fretted flats to the pier and the harbour. Far over the expanses of glowing burnt sienna mud, a growth of luminous and tawny rice grass is blocked in as if with a palette knife. The same sea-gulls perch top-heavy upon the white stakes that mark the estuary's course; other waterfowl skim and scuttle across the marshes. Small sailing craft float past us, running before the wind on a wing of red, white or tan sail. There, as usual, comes the sailing dinghy *Seamew*; the dark boy in a white public school sweater at the tiller; with him the fair pigtailed girl in a green blazer: brother and sister, or maybe cousins, fortunate pair; and they are hero and heroine of an enthralling Book for Girls about a jolly pair of boy and girl chums, Jack and Peggy (Pegs), who charter a boat for the hols and have ripping adventures. They wave to us; we wave back: romantic moment. Receding, they stay fixed, an illustration, between blue water and blue sky, their crimson sail behind them. Till next summer, next summer . . .' (78).

But the summers eventually end in the one during which the war breaks out, and the pellucid vision of childhood, which can both understand and not understand the tall red-haired young women with their separate preoccupations, is clouded – 'I suppose I was just young enough. A few years more, and *idées reçues*, from cousins chiefly, and *Daily Mirror* serials, would have interposed between me and the subject' (61).

During the war (as described in the previous chapter) Miss Mildred Daintrey, the most important of the characters, unexpectedly gets married. Time, that had stood still in the childhood summers on the Island, is inexorably taking its course: 'I do not know how long it was after that – a year? – more? – the war was over – that my mother came to us with a serious face and a letter in her hand, edged with black, portentous. "Girls, you remember the Daintreys –" She looked and sounded terribly sorry' (87). Miss Mildred has died and – true to a Lehmann preoccupation with water – been buried at sea.

'We were all very sorry; but we were growing up now; the Daintreys belonged to our childhood and had grown a little dim' (89). The deaths of the elderly Daintrey parents and the likely or possible future lives of the other members of the clan are briefly indicated, but 'the curtain falls' on them. As previously quoted, the story ends 'There will be no more families in England like the Daintrey family' (90).

The First World War, and the social changes it wrought forever, strike a subdued but consistent note in the background to all Rosamond Lehmann's books. I have already noted (Chapter II) its presence in *Dusty Answer* and also, though less markedly, in *Invitation to the Waltz*. That book, though published in 1932, is supposed to be taking place in 1920, a time when the full, long-term effects of the war, material and psychological, had yet to be plumbed. In its sequel, however (published in 1936 but apparently taking place about 1930) the war is, paradoxically, mentioned more. Or rather, it has by this time become something of a symbol and a shorthand way of referring to a sequence of change in Britain which, consequential on the war or not, was widely perceived to be so in the 1930s. This theme is formalised early on in *The Weather in the Streets* in a conversation Olivia has at the Spencer dinner party with an aged diplomat, father of the unsatisfactory Archie. Her admiration for the dining-room in which they are sitting provokes from him a lament for these country houses of Britain – then indeed very much in their last era as private homes:

[. . .] 'Look at Holkhurst! Look at Hilton! Closed free-quarters of ve year!'
  She hazarded tentatively:
  'I suppose it's the end of a chapter . . .?'
  'Yes, ve end of a chapter! Ve end of all aesfetic standards! I ask myself: who'll care a hundred years from now for art and letters . . .? I ask myself who . . .? [. . .] One must try to take ve long view – ve historical perspective . . . But what goes to my heart' – he leaned to her and muttered – 'is to see *vem* so hard up. It does indeed. Ve worry tells on vem. Vey put a brave face on it but ve worry tells. It's told on him.' He jerked his monocle in the direction of Sir John.
  'I'm afraid it has . . . An estate like this must be a terrible problem these days.'
  'Parting wiv ve Rembrandt was a terrible blow. And heaven knows what'll have to go next!' Another jerk, towards Rollo. 'What's to happen in his time I can't imagine. Unless he contrives to make some money. He's very able – oh, very able . . . Of course, a – an advantageous marriage would have helped matters, but vere it is . . . We couldn't wish vat uvverwise. Wiv a young man of his mettle, ve highest fings come first [. . .]' (84–5).

Rollo, as he has told Olivia in the train at their initial re-meeting, has resigned his Army commission (the traditional light occupation for a young man of the landed gentry) and has gone 'into the City' – presumably, since he does not say, stockbroking. He tells Olivia, 'It's the only way that presented itself to me of turning a necessary penny' (17). Affluent as he subsequently seems to the impoverished Olivia (who appears to live mainly on one of those tiny inter-war private incomes that upper middle-class families then still settled on their female members) it is significant that he has in effect abandoned his upper-class heritage to join the money-making bourgeoisie. The same is true of Hugh in *A Note in Music*: he is working in his uncle's shipping firm, yet his gold cigarette-case has engraved inside it '*Hugh George Miller, Esq. Presented by the Tenants of the Willowfields Estate on the occasion of his Twenty-first Birthday*' (129). The point is not explored – nothing is explored quite fully enough in this book – the family estate is still apparently there and flourishing. However, in *The Echoing Grove*, the same syndrome in Rickie Masters has reached a decisive outcome. Rickie works (again) in the shipping firm of some relative, and in the Second World War is plausibly translated to the Admiralty, but he is 'irrevocably out of the top-drawer'.

'What I mean was,' said Dinah [. . .] 'it must have been more of a wrench for Rickie than we realised, selling up his estates and going into business. He'd been brought up to be landed gentry like his fathers. It was a whole way of life gone – not just his own personal one: all his racial memories, you might call them. He couldn't have helped feeling he was letting down a lot of people – tenants and retainers – shirking his responsibilities. One shouldn't under-estimate that sort of dislocation' (154).

This, then, is the background in Lehmann-land against which the Second World War finally comes. 'When the Waters Came', the third story in *The Gipsy's Baby* collection, is set in the bad winter of 1939-40 during the period of the 'Phoney War', when hostilities had been declared but most of the action was still in abeyance. The scene is conveyed in a hyper-characteristic image:

'The war sprawled everywhere inert: like a child too big to get born it would die in the womb and be shovelled underground, disgracefully, as monsters are, and after a while, with returning health and a change of scene, we would forget that we conceived it' (93).

But, as the reader already knows, the enormity of full-scale war, *was* going to be fully born. This story (beginning 'Very long ago, during the first winter of the present war') is retrospective. It is an examination, via a domestic drama in the February floods, of a family on the brink of a catastrophe that they will nevertheless, probably, survive. ('What will the spring bring? Shall we be saved?' – 98).

In the next story, 'A Dream of Winter', the war is barely referred to, yet it is unmistakably present in the assumptions the story makes and the symbolism it suggests. As in 'When the Waters Came', a dramatic and alarming extreme of weather stands as proxy for the unseen war. It begins:

'In the middle of the great frost she was in bed with influenza; and that was the time the bee man came from the next village to take the swarm that had been for years buried in the wall of her country house; deep under the leads roofing the flat platform of the balcony outside her bedroom window' (101).

The symbolism of the swarm-taking and the honey the bees may or may not have stored there is explored with unusual fullness: more often Rosamond Lehmann's symbols are fleeting, dissolved in the action rather than at the centre of it. Here, the bee man's assault on the house's inner structure is perceived as some assault being made – by the war? Or by time itself? – on the fabric of the central character's life and hence on herself, at a moment when she is particularly weak (ill): 'A sense of terror overcame her, as if some dreaded exploratory physical operation of doubtful issue, and which she would be forced to witness, were about to take place. This growth was deep down in the body of the house. The waves of fever started to beat up again' (103).

A honeycomb is found. But –

'Dry, see,' said the bee man. 'You won't get much honey out of here.It's all that wet last summer. If I'd "a" taken this swarm a year ago, you'd "a" got a whole heap. You won't get anythink to speak of out of here now.'

She saw now: the papery transparent aspect of these ethereal growths meant a world extinct. She shivered violently, her spirit overwhelmed by symbols of frustration. Her dream had been rich: of honey pouring bountifully out from beneath her roof tree, to be stored up in family jugs, in pots and bowls, to spread on the bread and sweeten the puddings, and save herself a little longer from having to tell the children: No more sugar (105).

Ostensibly realistic and prosaic (sugar was increasingly tightly rationed during the Second World War) other layers of meaning are readily apparent. The 'wet last summer', with its suggestion of tears, seems to evoke a crisis and an echo of regret that some action had not been taken before. The 'ethereal growths . . . a world extinct' suggest a dead way of life – or perhaps a dead relationship. The honey itself 'pouring bountifully out from beneath her roof tree' obviously stands for some nourishing spirit of family life, some accreted emotional or spiritual sustenance built up by the past which has now been dissipated or spoiled. A paragraph or so later these private meanings merge into a less personal but still more coherent dread about the social changes the war was bringing:

Her Enemy, so attentive since the outbreak of the war, whispered in her ear:

'Just as I thought. Another sentimental illusion. Schemes to produce food by magic strokes of fortune. Life doesn't arrange stories with happy endings any more, see? *Never again*. This source of energy whose living voice comforted you at dawn, at dusk, saying: We work for you. Our surplus is yours, there for the taking – vanished! You left it to accumulate, thinking: There's time; thinking: when I will. You left it too late. What you took for the hum of growth and plenty is nothing, you see, but the buzz of an outworn machine running down. The workers have eaten up their fruits, there's nothing left for you. It's no use this time, my girl! Supplies are getting scarce for people like you. An end, soon, of getting more than their fair share for dwellers in country houses. Ripe gifts unearned out of traditional walls, no more [. . .]' (106).

We seem to be here with Olivia in the moments – only occasional ones – when she listens to her friend Jocelyn: 'You make me sit quiet and consider ideas – that injustice matters and unemployment, and the power and hypocrisy of rulers . . .' (*The Weather in the Streets*, 182). The left-wing views that had been the orthodoxy of a significant but numerically tiny intellectual minority in the 1930s had, under the pressures of war, been institutionalised into a generalised sense of inevitable democracy, conceded to even by those with no natural inclinations toward socialism whatsoever. This is the mental territory of Cyril Connolly's wartime classic of nostalgia and regret, *The Unquiet Grave*, and indeed of Evelyn Waugh's immediately post-war *Brideshead Revisited*, with its undisputed assumption that a cultured and comfortable way of life has gone forever. In fact, as we now know, this assumption was far too extreme. But the point is that it was being almost universally made in the middle of the war, and anyone of any sensitivity was aware of it and to some extent influenced by it, regardless of their own natural bent. The central character of the story we are discussing is socially 'placed' for us with a deprecating irony: 'She had a lot of leisure in her life to look at faces. She had friends with revolutionary ideas, and belonged to the Left Book Club' (103).

Quintessential Lehmann-woman, indeed. Rosamond Lehmann's novels all display an abiding readiness to be concerned about unfortunate individuals and a total absence of

the kind of organised political thinking that can express itself
as a View. (Dinah's strident left-wing views in *The Echoing
Grove* are seen entirely from the outside, as one might regard
an incomprehensible religious fervour, or indeed as Rosamond
Lehmann regarded Wogan Philipps' conversion to Communism.) One or two inquisitive observers of her life, noting that
she and Goronwy Rees had a brief association at the time her
marriage was breaking up, have made assumptions about her
interest in politics, or even her inside knowledge of the left-
wing machinations then in progress – assumptions which
are, in my view, totally unwarranted. Indeed the absolute
divergence of her own political attitudes from the left-wing
ones espoused by her husband were, according to her, a major
factor in the final collapse of her marriage. She was, she says,
sympathetic to the Communist cause in Spain against Franco,
but *not* with Communism as such.

To return to the story: honey *is* discovered after all in the
roof beams. But – further symbolism – it has been there
too long and is spoiled. The two children, John and Jane –
undisguised portraits of the author's children Hugo and Sally
– invade the bedroom with their disappointment: ' "It isn't
delicious. It's beastly. It looks like seccotine and it tastes *much*
too sweet. Ugh!" ' (110).

The story ends with a different image, curious but pregnant.
The children have rescued a bird brought in by a cat. They
bring it up to show it to their mother, and it flies straight into
the fireplace:

In a split second she was there, plunged in her hand, out again. Smell
of burnt feathers, charred fragments flaking down. It was on the
hearth-stone. Everybody started.

Suddenly it revived, it began to stagger about. The tenacity of life
in its minute frame appalled her. Over the carpet it bounced, one
wing burnt off, one leg shrivelled up under its breast, no tail; up and
down, vigorously, round and about.

'Is it going to be alive?' said Jane.

'Yes,' said John coldly, heavily. 'We can't do anything about it now' (111-12).

An appalling message of both hope and dread. Perhaps the central character does not entirely *want* to go on. But in spite of her apparent fragility of spirit she is a survivor, she must. In any case, significantly, it was she whose instinctual action retrieved the bird from the brink of death.

This image of Lehmann-woman as someone of competence-notwithstanding is present in all three of the Second World War stories, and particularly in the last and longest one, 'Wonderful Holidays'. This enchanting and deceptively simple account covers a few days not long before D-day, when a rather older John and Jane and a neighbouring family of similar ages are putting on a fund-raising show in the Village Hall; it catches the essence of wartime family and local life. It is 1944, doom has receded after all, the war will be won, and Lehmann-woman, like all her contemporaries, is deeply involved in providing food, caring for her young and co-operating willy-nilly in that patriotic exercise known in war as 'doing her bit'. The aspect of her that smoked too much and sat alone in a bedsitter 'wondering what the people were like who lived in the room before me; dead now . . .' (*The Weather in the Streets*, 201) is in eclipse; instead we ac-company her as she discusses arrangements with her children, fields the vicar on the telephone – ('"You encourage him," said John. "I do not. I can't discourage him: that's quite another matter. You must learn to be more accurate"' – 127) – and successfully retrieves Jane's school trunk, missing for ten days on the railway. She even manages to cook lunch for a neighbour, Captain Moffat, one of those damaged survivors of the last war that haunt the pages of the Lehmann novels. This sets off in her a wave of fantasy about how Captain Moffat and his wife might yet be encouraged into a richer life, perhaps even into having a child (like blinded Timmy in the Olivia books, who is similarly married to a Molly); only then does a pang of introspective suffering surface:

She checked her step sharply, and said aloud: 'Really, you're revolting.' Still this sickening self-indulgent day-dreaming, this perpetual wash of emotional flotsam, blocking the channels of the clear flow of reason. No ideas, no intellectual progress, none. No wonder, perhaps, that Charles her husband had left her years ago, transferring his suitcases, his typewriter, his notes for a book on Marxist aesthetics and his affections to a clear-browed female research student in physics (147-8).

But 'Mrs Ritchie' (as she is called in this story) is rescued from her endemic grief by the immediate need to attend to something else – the rehearsal with a neighbouring lady, Mrs Carmichael, of a sketch they are contributing to the Show. And there is a conjuror to organise: will the one Mrs Carmichael has tracked down do? '"He sounded – sort of *old* [. . .] I think," said Mrs Carmichael, "he was *drunk*"' (148). And, drunk or sober, how is he to come and go from the village?

'I've told him to take the last bus out from Brading. But getting him *back* is another matter. If we could get him down to Redbury he could catch a train – if there is one. I wonder if Turnbull would come and fetch him. I suppose I'd better find out at once.'

She went away to telephone, and shortly returned saying: 'Mr Turnbull says he'd oblige if he could but it's his fire-watching night, and if it turned out to be the – you know – *the* night, and he was to be absent from his post even for half an hour, you can imagine the results. How comforting it is when powerful things like garages and coal-merchants don't refuse you with gloating glee. It sets one up almost as much as if they'd said yes.' With a return of her natural buoyancy, she examined her pretty face in a pocket mirror, re-decorated her mouth and said: 'Oh well, if the worst comes to the worst, one of us will have to put him up. I wouldn't really mind, would you? He might be so interesting.'

'I'd mind terribly. And so would he. I'm sure it would be against the rules of the Magician's Union. And don't you dare even hint such a possibility in front of the children, or we shall get no peace. Come on, we'd better run through our parts before they get back' (150).

It is the authentic note of 1944: apparently casual, parochial, self-mocking – but with a constant undercurrent of expectation, like a low hum, lending a degree of excitement and tension to the most tedious wartime chores: *the* night (D-day) is known to be coming. (The 'Wonderful Holidays' of the title are the Spring holidays, probably late April: D-day turned out to be 6 June.)

The story falls into two parts. The first is taken up with the varied daily activities and the preparations for the Show: the second by the Show itself and the Ritchie-Carmichael party afterwards. Right at the end of the first part appears a character, already much-mentioned by the worshipping Jane, who will be the most significant figure for Mrs Ritchie in the second part: he is an Etonian friend of the Carmichael boys, but readers of Rosamond Lehmann have met him before, in many guises. He is the wonderful young man, now less of a lover-figure than a son:

Roger Wickham, tall, slight, walking with the uncertain grace of his eighteen years, came through the trees towards them, carrying a huge sheaf of flowering cherry branches. He had a pale long cool-looking face, a fine head covered with wavy light-brown hair, beautiful secretive lips and clear eyes like aquamarines. They all looked at him smiling, and he smiled back, looking at none of them.

'I picked these for you,' he said, dividing his sheaf, giving half to Mrs Carmichael, and half to Mrs Ritchie (155-6).

We might almost be back in *Dusty Answer* – a novel in which a cherry tree, incidentally, plays an emblematic part. But the world of 'Wonderful Holidyas' is based in reality, not in the theme of illusion, and for the rest of the story Roger occupies the convincing rôle of charming, gifted but real young man. He plays the violin at the Village Hall for communal singing – a lord of the manor delightfully entertaining the tenantry. Later, at the party, he dances with Mrs Ritchie. They talk about people still dancing in London in spite of the war, about painting – he is an amateur artist as well as violinist. She says:

'You're going to go on with it? Make it your career?'

'I don't know. I do wonder.' He sounded impersonal, incurious. 'I'm in hot water all round at present. My Papa destines me for the family business. He doesn't care to see me idling about and fiddling with brushes. He's worried. Mr Carrington's worried too. I appear to be stuck. My report says: Unable to finish anything. What is to be done?'

'It's just one of those bad patches. They're inevitable. You'll make a big step forward soon.' But she felt at a loss. What intuition, what secret principle was at work within him? What moved him? He was without ambition. Delightful dilettante, would he come to nothing?

[. . .] She said, feeling shy: 'Perhaps you'd come and stay with us some time. We'd all love it.'

'How very kind of you. That would be delightful. There's nothing I'd like better.' The tune died away. The voice of Renaldo himself came on the air, crooned out a personal good-night. It was midnight. 'Unfortunately,' said Roger, 'the shades of the prison house will have closed on me by the summer. I shall be in the Army.'

'In the Army? As soon as that. I forgot. You're eighteen?'

'Eighteen last month.'

'Are you dreading it?'

'Oh, no.' He nodded. 'I'm rather looking forward to it.'

He would go into the Army, and be drilled and do fatigues and go on courses, and be sent to his OCTU and get his commission, and have embarkation leave and vanish from England under security silence and . . . come to nothing?

'Perhaps the war will end,' she said.

She looked at him. He looked away over the room, smiling secretively. What was his meaning? 'You see, as things are, it's rather pointless really, isn't it, to commit myself, to choose, to have a future . . .' Was that it? Or had he no meaning? (188–9).

This is the darkest touch in this otherwise gay and extrovert tale. One's reaction is that the sense of imminent doom, the cutting off of a life just beginning to flower, is more closely derived from the First World War than the Second – that it is indeed an integral part of the wonderful-young-man syndrome in the author's consciousness. I should also add, however, that years after the story was written the person on whom (according to Rosamond Lehmann) Roger Wickham was to some extent based, committed suicide. This is not the only occasion in her works where the theme of pre-recognition seems to surface, fugitive and unexplored.

But in 'Wonderful Holidays' the touch is of the lightest. Even the irony that murder is the game played by the children at the party only strikes the reader afterwards. Although the subjective vision is that of Mrs Ritchie, the voices of the children dominate the scene and much of what happens is filtered to the reader through their perception of it. In particular Jane (Rosamond's own daughter Sally at the age of about ten) is the prevailing spirit, a combination of archetypal child and unique individual:

The front door banged, shutting off Mr and Mrs Carmichael. Feet pounded down the darkness and away. Shouts, laughter diminished in the distance. Mrs Ritchie grasped Jane to her side. They found themselves alone in the drive.

'Where've they gone?' said Jane, dazed, walking at her mother's side.

'Only just a little way up the lane with Puffles. You heard them say they'd be back very soon.'

'Did John go? And Audrey? Why couldn't I go? They went without telling me.'

'Oh darling, it's nothing to miss. Just groping about in that pitch-dark muddy old lane. You wouldn't have enjoyed it a bit.'

'Did Meg go?'

'No, no. I'm sure Meg's going to bed this very moment.'

'I thought I saw her dash out of the door.'

'No.' Mrs Ritchie suppressed an identical image.

'I'll ask her tomorrow. Did John ask you if he could go?'

'No, he didn't. He's a bad boy and I'm cross with him.'

'I wouldn't have thought Audrey would go without asking.'

The face of Audrey at the door came before Mrs Ritchie; sparkling, eager, lost to decorum. 'I bet they won't come back for hours.'

Only too likely. She saw them ranging the countryside with whoop and chorus. I won't have it, she told herself, furious, impotent.

'Darling,' she said, 'I'm glad you stayed with me. I should have been sad going home alone.'

Jane pressed her hand. They crossed the lane and climbed the steep withy bank into the pasture, where open space made a faint lightening of the deep darkness.

'We forgot to bring a torch,' said Jane. 'Never mind. I like being out at night with you. Walking, walking in nowhere. It doesn't seem as if we were in the world at all.' She squeezed her hand tightly again.

'Oh Jane, I haven't danced for years. Not since you were born' (190-91).

For the reader of today, an extra dimension is added to this tender picture of mother-daughter intimacy – a relationship which Rosamond Lehmann has described elsewhere as 'the deepest listening of my life' (*The Swan in the Evening*, 95). For, as is well known, Sally, who grew into a gifted and much loved adult, died suddenly of poliomyelitis in the Far East in 1958, when she was twenty-three. Her mother's belief in the continuance of that 'listening' has dominated and transformed the later part of her own life.

But it would be a mistake to take the realistic, almost documentary surface of 'Wonderful Holidays' as complete evidence for Rosamond Lehmann's life during the early forties of the century and of her own life. Her life in the country with her children was only one aspect of her existence. Children of that class were then sent to boarding school almost as a matter of course, and during their school terms their mother had another life, much of it elsewhere. This was shared with Cecil Day Lewis, the poet and publisher, who was married himself and whom Rosamond Lehmann had first met in Elizabeth

Bowen's flat in 1936. In April 1941 they re-met – according to Sean Day-Lewis, Cecil's son:

After a chance re-union during one of the spring blitzes he had fallen in love with Rosamond Lehmann and had not been rejected. Neither she nor he recorded dates or addresses and it is not possible to be altogether precise about the when and where of this all-consuming nine-year relationship: so important to Cecil for his development both as a poet and as a person; so important to Rosamond that in her vulnerable forties she unwisely and generously committed her whole heart to him. All that can be said for certain is that before the end of the year they were living together in Kensington, the first of several houses around London where they found time to be together, and Cecil had embarked on his period of 'double marriage', 'sweet influences' and 'a stress such as I had never known'. (*Cecil Day Lewis: An English Literary Life.*)

Meanwhile Cecil's wife, Mary, was herself living as a war-time, country housewife, with other children in another village. The triangular relationship, which had already figured in *Dusty Answer* (Judith, Jennifer, Geraldine) and in *The Weather in the Streets*, seems to have been one of those constants in Rosamond Lehmann's mental landscape which, at intervals, surfaced inexorably in her life as well as her books. It was to achieve its full-scale fictional treatment in *The Echoing Grove* (1953). Like all Rosamond Lehmann's novels, this one undoubtedly owes something to events in her own life in the preceding years. And yet, again like all her novels, the essential themes – love, conflict, betrayal, divided loyalties – seem to have been there from the beginning.

CHAPTER VIII

Mothers

I have already commented on the distinctive rôle played in Rosamond Lehmann's books by the father: almost, in folklore terms, a king-must-die rôle in order that the woman should be freed to love another. I have said less till now about the mothers in her work, and indeed some of the references to the mother in the short stories and in the Olivia books might give the impression that Lehmann-mother is something of a stock figure, household linchpin, whose main literary function is to act as a counterpoint to the passion and disorder created by her young. But such an impression is false: although the various Mrs Landon-Ellison-Curtis characters *do* play this rôle, essentially for Rosamond Lehmann the mother figure has much additional significance and importance. It was obviously not by chance that the birth of the daughter ('what I longed for') was the start of what was arguably *the* major relationship of her life: such a sense of instant commitment – 'recognition' – could only have been based on intense previous experience of the mother-daughter tie. Not that the mothers and daughters in Lehmann-land appear greatly in sympathy with one another's views, any more than Mrs R. C. Lehmann and her second daughter often agreed on the proper conduct of life. But emotional involvement is certainly present.

Not till *The Echoing Grove* does this fine but tough thread between mother and adult daughter surface as a fully-realised theme in its own right. Meanwhile, I mention it as one of the elements – but only one – apparently fuelling the emotional message of that strange, compelling book *The Ballad and the Source*, which some consider to be Rosamond Lehmann's finest work, some consider melodramatic and artificial, but which all concede to be the most unexpected she ever wrote.

It is possible, indeed, to see *The Ballad and the Source* almost entirely in terms of the mother-daughter relationship, in its most primeval and daunting form. An American commentator, Sydney Jane Kaplan, has written a paper on this theme entitled: 'Rosamond Lehmann's The Ballad and the Source: a Confrontation with "The Great Mother"' (*Twentieth Century Literature*, June 1982, Hofstra University Press, N.Y.), and while I believe her thesis, on close examination, to be substantially false, I cite it here as an interesting example of the way the fragile structure of *The Ballad and the Source* can, in general terms, raise the shadows of some of the basic myths of humankind. Ms Kaplan relates the whole novel to the Demeter myth – the goddess of fertility frantically seeking and finally regaining the daughter that the God of the Underworld, the destructive male principle, has stolen and ravished. But since the Demeter-Persephone myth is characterised by the primordial and unbreakable bond between mother and daughter (something of obvious appeal to feminists), and the mother-daughter relations in *The Ballad and the Source* are characterised, over two generations, by the striking absence of any such bond and by *maternal* destructiveness, this particular myth would seem of only limited relevance. What is, however, undoubtedly true is that the main character, Sibyl Jardine, from her name onwards, does embody many of the two-edged qualities of the archetypal Great Mother-Terrible Mother. What is more to the point is that *she* sees herself as some sort of fertility principle, source of life and power – the source, indeed, of the title: '"The source, Rebecca! The fount of life – the source, the quick spring that rises in the illimitable depths of darkness and flows through every living thing from generation to generation. It is what we feel mounting in us when we say 'I know! I love! I am!'"' (101).

But – and this is a main theme of the novel – Mrs Jardine is deluding herself, and expending a great deal of energy in deluding others, particularly the impressionable child Rebecca. Essentially this is one of those novels where the story is strained through the 'limited view' of one individual, but in which the adult reader sees more, and more clearly. As with Henry James' *What Maisie Knew*, there is constantly a gap between what the child – Rebecca – knows and hears and what we ourselves make of it. Mrs Jardine, whatever her original or potential gifts, is, by the time the book opens, a woman past her own time of creation and a *poseuse* on a massive scale. As another character (Gil, her last lover) remarks late in the book:

'From anybody else in the world [. . .] she gets back – *immeasurable* reflections of herself. It's not deliberate, so it's pointless to moralise about it: it's some property of her nature – some principle. Like yeast. She throws out all she has – her beauty, her gifts, her power over people – and objects – and events; and it works. Each time she tries it out, it works like magic. Up come all these disturbing, magnetised self-images [. . .]' (236–7).

But self-images are all that come up. The magic lies in the spinning of a romantic ballad in which she occupies the central rôle and which, like all good ballads – but not like most respected twentieth-century novels – contains a high component of drama, passion and romance. The source, in practice, is dry: Mrs Jardine is not a procreator but a destroyer. One may assume that she was herself the original victim, caught and deformed in a sickly marriage, but what then happens is that eventually she deserts and destroys her only daughter, who then, in turn, deserts her own children. Mrs Jardine tries to repossess her maternal heritage in the form of these three children, but by the end of the novel two of them are dead and the third is vowing to herself she will never fall in love or procreate since it leads to so much pain. A sexual creature Mrs Jardine is, but it is sterility, not fertility, that is the end-result of passion in her life, just as it is on a more realistic and understated plane in the lives of those other suffering, sexual creatures, Olivia Curtis in *The Weather in the Streets*, and Dinah and Georgie in *the Echoing Grove*. In living entirely on and for her own emotions, Sibyl Jardine is like a monstrous distortion of what Lehmann-woman, without her other human attributes, might become. She is certainly huge and powerful as a character (Rosamond Lehmann: 'She just became *enormous*') but she is a hollow one, and I must confess I find it hard to see why some readers have felt so essentially powerless a character to be 'frightening', as they apparently have. It is surely significant that Rebecca's real mother (who has a minor but distinct rôle in the novel) is not in the least impressed by the Mythic Mother Goddess in the fairytale house on the hill, and that this point is made from the start. Mrs Landon has received a letter from Mrs Jardine (who has newly returned from abroad) inviting Rebecca, Jess and Sylvia to tea:

[. . .] '*Precarious health has prostrated me at intervals for the last twenty years: but who knows? – this may prove to be the right spot. I have liked to think of the children coming each year with primrose baskets to the hill. They have often appeared to me, like dreams, like images in poetry . . .*' My mother stopped, raised her eyebrows. Her expression was complex.

'Go on,' I said.

'Hmm – hmm – *like poetry – spirit-like, unreal, yet in another sense so real – coming, for me, from so far back in the past, linked to what is clearest and most cherished in my memory – promising me something still to come, as it were, out of the past, into the present and future, in this spring primrose-picking . . . Little Primaveras . . .* Primavera was the Goddess of Spring,' said my mother, deprecating all this, but improving the occasion. 'There's a very famous picture of her by – er – by a great Italian painter' (6).

In the next few pages it becomes clear – at any rate to the adult reader – that Mrs Jardine's past includes a friendship with the children's grandmother that was terminated abruptly and something in the nature of a romantic relationship with the children's father.

I might say in passing that an objective source for Sibyl Jardine is hard to locate – apparently even for her creator. In *The Swan in the Evening*, as one example of the simplistic 'character-spotting' to which she feels she has been subjected, Rosamond Lehmann remarks:

'A character called Mrs Jardine that I once created, generated from a fusion of youthful impressions of relatives on the paternal side, has had five different "real life" models attached to her, all ludicrously wide of the mark, three of them unknown to me even by repute' (67). Elaborating slightly on this, she has told me that, two generations back in Rudolf Lehmann's family, there had been a woman who had left her husband and small child for another man and was afterwards prevented, according to the *mores* of the period, from seeing her child – the original sin that Sibyl Jardine commits and from which all the rest follows. Rosamond Lehmann herself knew this cousin in old age, and was even drawn at one point into the cousin's scheme for getting her child back. She was a writer and a traveller, apparently a magnetic, quintessentially untruthful person – a 'self-deceiver of enormous proportions', – though with 'great gifts of affection': and the young Rosamond Lehmann was fascinated by her. But the physical model whom she 'saw' when writing *The Ballad and the Source* was not this relation but another, a much more benign figure whom she did in fact love: her father's sister. And in any case, when starting what she thought was going to be a story but what developed into a novel, her original thought was that behind the secret walled garden of the 'house on the hill' her children would find the real occupant of such a house that she had in fact known – 'a darling old lady in a wheelchair, crippled with arthritis.'

In other words, the white witch-fairy godmother revealed

herself, on closer examination, as a wicked witch as well. That is probably as far as we can or should pursue the sources of fiction into the unconscious – Rosamond Lehmann herself says that, interesting as she finds speculation about Jungian archetypes in her work, she herself was almost entirely un-aware of them at the time of writing. But the garden of the house on the hill, to which the children subsequently come often to play with Mrs Jardine's grandchildren, is so important a component in the scene-setting of the book that it may be instructive to compare it with another faintly magic garden, in *A Note in Music*. This is the place where Grace, Norah and several other characters spend the one happy and revelatory day of the whole book, and significantly it too contains 'a darling old lady' with a handicap (deafness). Like a sybil, she sits embroidering – but, like Mrs Jardine, who was not to be created for the best part of fifteen years, she has a Past. '"She had lovers, I suppose you know: or at least a lover"' her grandson tells Norah, his cousin. However this Mother God-dess appears to have been more fortunate than Sibyl Jardine, since the grandson continues: '"I don't know how they ar-ranged the offspring question, but I presume they had an understanding. At any rate, my father was reared under the label of Seddon"' (156). And Norah thinks a few pages later – 'She had known everybody – sailing through the worlds both of society and of social rebels in some astonishing and successful way of her own' (173).

The picture is rather a facile one – evading, one might say, the whole topic of ageing beauty, past sexuality, which *The Ballad and the Source* was, in turn, to grasp almost too ferociously, and without regard for the bathos of reality. It would have been interesting to see this pregnant and little-explored topic figure further in Rosamond Lehmann's novels, but in *The Echoing Grove* it is broached only as a horror-element (Madeleine's agony when, in middle age, she is deserted by her lover), and in any case one of the curious characteristics of this book (see Chapter x) is that in its present-time sections both Madeleine and Dinah seem older than their chronological ages, as if more years had passed than can actually have been the case. The novel in which one might have expected the whole question of age and femaleness to come up for review is *A Sea-Grape Tree* (1976), but while, in this belated novel, Mrs Jardine actually makes a spectral appearance, the tale is set back to the 1930s and Rebecca is therefore still a young woman. It is, in any case, a novel that seems more concerned with dreams and wish-fulfilment than with the tenacious pursuit of truth that characterised much of Rosamond Lehmann's earlier work.

I have already mentioned (Chapter 1) the importance of place as an element in Rosamond Lehmann's creative inspiration. The attentive reader will recognise the house on the hill of *the Ballad and the Source* as playing something the same rôle, as a focus for romance and interest, that the house next door did in *Dusty Answer*, or indeed the big house where the Spencers lived. But there is another location which seems to have been a departure point for *The Ballad and the Source*: for once the author herself identified it, in an article on 'The Future of the Novel' she wrote for *Britain Today* in 1946:

'. . . a portion of a little French river choked with water lilies, with a weir on it and an inn on its banks, which for some inexplicable reason impressed itself upon my imagination years ago as the place where something that I would one day cause to happen, would happen; and from the image (whose origins are lost to me) of a woman's figure in a blue cloak.'

The French location, with the weir and the inn, figures in the the final, most dramatic part of the saga – as recounted to Rebecca by Mrs Jardine's granddaughter. The woman in the blue cloak is Sibyl Jardine herself, appearing in the park many years before to gaze from afar at her estranged child; and again at the very end of the book in a frightening dream, not a person but a spectre, an embodiment of some dreadful adult truth. Or is she? Rosamond Lehmann herself wrote in 1931 (*A Letter to a Sister*, Hogarth Press): 'Society isn't what it was. Surely it has lost its glamour in the nursery; the thrill of virtue and wickedness is less, rewards and punishments are out of fashion.' A problem with this novel is that a reader who does not instinctively empathise with Rebecca's Edwardian child's-eye view of Mrs Jardine will find the whole artefact, recitative narrative-technique and all, hard to take. A number of reviewers, when it came out toward the end of the Second World War, did indeed regard it as a piece of work without relevence or importance – one American reviewer, under the heading 'Edwardian tremulo', called it 'an invitation to nostalgia'. Other readers, however, including some of the author's friends, seem to have revelled in the very romantic, baroque nature of the work, as a feast for the spirit at a time of austerity, rations and rationalism, and intense practical pressures.

More perceptively, Diana Trilling wrote, in *The Nation*:

'It is a psychological mystery of the type Henry James delighted in, and from the precocious child who sees and hears such a large part of the story, through the careful architecture of the narrative and its emphasis on psychological motive, to the atmosphere of well-bred horror, *The Ballad and the Source* reveals its distinguished ancestry. Even the names of the characters suggest the connection' (April 1945).

She is referring here to the fact that Mrs Jardine's older granddaughter is called Maisie. One may be tempted to compare Tilly's dead son 'the little Feller' (see below) with Mrs Wix's dead Clara Matilda in *What Maisie Knew* – and indeed the grandchildrens' Auntie Mack and Mrs Wix herself. Literary echoes seem to abound in this novel, and at moments the whole thing appears to partake of a literary convention that must be called Jamesian but sometimes seems closer to the artificial conventions of the detective story. Rosamond Lehmann wrote the book during her long involvement with Cecil Day Lewis and while he, under the name Nicholas Blake, was writing detective stories: she herself rather disliked his Blake books, and would repudiate any suggestion of influence. It is not, therefore, to make any conclusive point that I indicate the coincidence of the stone heads, which more than one reader has pointed out to me. In *The Ballad and the Source* Gil, a sculptor, has sculpted some heads that are perceived by the mad Ianthe (Mrs Jardine's daughter) as the real thing. Four years later, Cecil Day Lewis, alias Nicholas Blake, published a crime story, *The Head of a Traveller*, set in a country house in Oxfordshire, in which a similar confusion between a real head and a modelled one occurs, and in which moreover the central character is a highly powerful and amoral middle-aged woman. Influence would therefore seem to have passed, if at all, *from* Rosamond Lehmann to her companion – but the subject of literary influence is a highly complex one.

On the whole, I have found that those who respond empathetically to *The Ballad and the Source* do not respond particularly to the other novels, and vice versa. It is a measure of its popularity, in some spheres, that in 1947 the film rights were sold. The film was never made – probably fortunately, since the eye of the camera would surely have penetrated the novel's fragile structure and demolished it. But, with the substantial sum of the money from the sale of the rights, Rosamond Lehmann bought a Georgian manor at Little Wittenham, Berkshire. This was intended to be a home for herself and Cecil Day Lewis as well as her children. But two years later, it was to become the scene of their agonised and bitter last encounter. There seems a terrible symbolism in the fact that such a novel should, in the long run, bring its author nothing good.

However, no serious student of Rosamond Lehmann's work can fail to be interested, at least, by many aspects of *the Ballad and the Source*, and in particular by the way in which some of the basic images of Lehmann-land surface as constantly as ever, even in this baroque construction. Most notably, there is the youngest granddaughter, Cherry, who dies of meningitis despite all Mrs Jardine's obsessional efforts to seize and keep her for her own. A particular pathos is added to this by the detail that Cherry has been something of a Victorian child, delicate, spending days in bed, or perhaps with a changeling element about her, playing at death in life:

[. . .] A mad notion pierced me: Cherry was about to come in. Till this moment, I had suppressed the image of the third, the absent one; but now she rose up, sucking her finger, inserting herself obliquely in quarter-opened doorways, hovering, sidling and twining there, nagging for attention; then at first sign of Maisie's awaited pounce, withdrawing with noiseless rapidity and prolonged nerve-rattling exhibitions of mystification on the door-handle, from the other side. 'Take no notice,' Maisie would hiss. 'She wants us to think it's a blasted ghost.' With terror I thought that if I were to go out now and search through the fabulous shrubbery, I should come upon one of those match-boxes stuffed with scraps of moss, leaf, berry, petal which she delighted to hide there, in mouse-scale nooks and crannies (226).

There is a hint – no more than a hint – that Cherry is a child of adultery, half-sister only to the more prosaic Maisie and Malcolm. Everyone wants her – Mrs Jardine and teenage Maisie, who engage in a covert and bitter battle over her, and Harry Jardine, her step-grandfather; in thematic terms, it is inevitable she should die. Harry Jardine, Mrs Jardine's second husband, is incidentally another of those constant inhabitants of Lehmann-land: he is an ex-soldier who has suffered some fearful damage, visible or invisible, and he is an inadequate husband-figure (see Captain Moffat in 'Wonderful Holidays'). His own strength lies in some form of passive, subversive

resistance to his wife, under cover of adoration. Mrs Jardine
consistently presents him as a man of enormous, if retiring
qualities; Rebecca observes that there is something odd about
him; to the adult reader he is clearly an alcoholic – further
evidence of Mrs Jardine's power to spread sterility and death.
Another damaged father-figure is embodied in the grandchildren's actual father, who dies off-stage in the course of the
novel – in Newcastle, forever the Bleak Place of exile for
Rosamond Lehmann! The feeling about it is put into the
mouth of 'Auntie' Mack, the quintessential unmarried female
relative who keeps house for the children's father after his
wife, Ianthe, has deserted him: '"I am a country woman, born
and bred," she said. "For seven years I have looked out of sad
windows and seen rows of grey houses opposite, tram lines
between. I have waked to the clamour of the first tram and
laid my head down upon the pillow to the clang of the last
one . . ."' (184).

I have already mentioned Auntie Mack's general resemblance to Henry James's governess Mrs Wix: she seems indeed
more of a literary archetype – albeit an effective one, with her
indigestion, her Scottish accent and her desperate decency –
than a real person:

It was Auntie Mack, none other, who addressed these words to me
in a penetrating and genial whinny. A very large hand gripped mine
and wrung it hard. She was a tall, protuberant, bony person, with a
carelessly assembled frame. She was dressed in a black jacket and
skirt, both of unusual length, fusty, dusty, threadbare, trimmed with
wide black braid and voluminously flared below the waist and knees.
Her black blouse was secured at the throat by the largest cameo
brooch I have ever seen; and in addition she was hung with chains
of various sizes and designs. Her narrow flat chest broadened to an
abnormal convexity combined with meagreness in the hips. Her legs
and feet were elephantine. Her bundles of hair, striped sandy and
white, were done up askew in plaited circles secured by formidable
steel prongs. Desultory wisps hung round the expanse of her face

and forehead like a tacked-on oddment of frayed and faded trimming. She had a flourishing sandy moustache and long pinkish-yellow cheeks patched with freckles, bulging sad green eyes with white lashes, and a big solid yet somehow vacant assortment of features (182).

We have already met something like this caricature figure before in Rosamond Lehmann's work during the 1940s: Mildred Daintrey –

the family's chief prop and right hand, the unselfish one. She had a particularly large white face, narrow at the brows, broadening out like a pear, with rather pendulous cheeks. She wore pince-nez, and behind them her protuberant green eyes gleamed out with emotional benevolence. There was something marine about her appearance: that faintly phosphorescent flesh colour, like legs under water; that globularly soulful quality of the faces of fishes, mooning out from behind aquarium glass. She was no longer young, though it would appear now that she cannot have been elderly, as then seemed obvious. Her hair was the most uncompromising, assertive red I have ever seen, and she wore it *en Pompadour*. The fact is, although she was so good and kind, that what with her height, her glasses, her phantasmagorical colouring, and her low, harsh, cockney-genteel voice, she was the picture of a horror-governess in a story by Mr de la Mare (*The Gipsy's Baby*, 59-60).

But the essential difference between 'The Red-haired Miss Daintreys' and *The Ballad and the Source* is that, in the former, Miss Mildred is set up as a literary convention *in order* to be gradually revealed as a unique individual with her own story and tragic stature, whereas Auntie Mack remains on a circus-act level, wheeled on to provide Rebecca with another view-point, another chapter in the saga, and then withdrawn, not to reappear. In the same way another memorable grotesque, Tilly, an elderly sewing maid in the Landon family who remembers Mrs Jardine as a young woman, is the central performer in the second section of the book, where she gives a dramatic monologue recounting what Rebecca's grandmother told her that Sibyl Jardine had told *her*. But once this *tour de force* is over Tilly has fulfilled her entire function in the novel and must be disposed of – indeed the point is made almost explicitly, in the opening of the next section:

Tilly left us a day or two later. She said she'd be more herself when she got back to her own place in London, where her landlady studied her ways and the girls were bright: it was the country made her feel low – she never could abear it. She was mulishly vacant, sullenly melancholy. My mother tried to persuade her to see the doctor, and after that Tilly refused to speak to her any more, and left without saying good-bye. There was nothing my mother could do except write to the landlady, asking to be kept informed of Tilly's condition, and offering any assistance within her power. We were relieved to see the dolman and bonnet disappearing round the bend of the garden path towards the station. The garden boy stumped ahead of her with her portmanteau; and that was the last we saw of her. She was not our Tilly any more; she was an inauspicious old fairy, ill-wishing our hearth. Unable to rid myself of the suspicion that my afternoon with her was responsible for her final disintegration, I felt a double relief at her departure (96).

She has been presented as a literary 'card' from the beginning –

a diminutive cockney, just not a dwarf, cased always from head to foot in glossy black, with a little lace-bordered black silk apron, jet ornaments and a cornelian brooch [. . .] Twice widowed before the age of thirty, she had married first one Mr Pringle, to whom in the course of interminable reminiscences she never once referred; next a handsome and romantic Bohemian cabinet-maker, by whom she had one son, know to us as the Little Feller. He had been all brains and no stamina, his little spine grew crooked and she lost him at the age of six (14).

In spite of the familiar dead-child motif, Tilly seems a pastiche figure, insufficiently conceived: indeed the author herself remarks dismissively that 'Her reality belonged entirely to the Dickens world' (14). It comes as something of a surprise to learn that she was based on one entirely real person, 'Dickie', the Lehmann-grandmother's old ladies' maid, who used to come down to Fieldhead to sew for months at a time when Rosamond and her sisters and brother were children. She had been married to a man called Dickinson and really had had a boy who had died in childhood. Her second husband had been a Bohemian cabinet-maker.

This faintly exploitative attitude to a number of her characters is elsewhere untypical of Rosamond Lehmann, one of whose many qualities as a novelist has been her ability to see beyond stereotypes. Perhaps one can only say that, given the particular narrative technique she employs in *The Ballad and the Source*, a degree of exploitation is inevitable, just as the 'artificiality' and 'improbability' with which this novel has also been charged is inevitable also. Obviously it is highly 'unlikely' by the reality standards of, say, *The Weather in the Streets*, or *The Echoing Grove*, that Tilly, Auntie Mack, Maisie, Gil or indeed Mrs Jardine herself, should have recounted so much, in such detail and at such length, with such total recall and often at one or even two removes from the original speaker, to an eleven- or twelve-year-old child. But such is the convention of this kind of psychological detective story, and it is a convention, incidentally, not confined to James, and one which others besides Rosamond Lehmann explored at that period. See Stefan Zweig's *Beware of Pity* (1939) for a successful and thorough-going use of it, or see *The House in Paris* (1934) by Rosamond Lehmann's friend and contemporary Elizabeth Bowen – a model very close in some respects to *The Ballad and the Source*, since the main listener is there too a child and what is gradually revealed is a comparable saga of past adult misdoings and maternal desertion. Yet there the revelation concerns the child more closely, seems less gratuitous.

Perhaps one of the most skilful aspects of *The Ballad and the Source* is its manipulation of the time-scale of events, and since the conveying of psychological time rather than actual time was to be one of the central qualities of *The Echoing Grove*, written some seven or eight years later, it is interesting to observe the way in which, in the apparently so-different *The Ballad and the Source*, the author was already exploring the possiblities of an elliptic method of construction. Early in the book the narrator (Rebecca as an adult) remarks: 'Looking back into childhood is like looking into a semi-transparent globe within which people and places lie embedded. A shake – and they stir, rise up, circle in inter-weaving groups, then settle down again. There are no dates. Time is not movement forward or backward through them, but simply that colourless globe in which they are all contained' (27). But in fact time does move in *The Ballad and the Source*, both past and present time, in a carefully orchestrated and inter-connected way.

When the novel opens, it is a couple of years before the First World War. We are apparently back on the far side of that great twentieth-century chasm, safe in a pre-war world, where children wear 'our navy blue serge sailor blouses and skirts and jackets with brass buttons, and set off after lunch accompanied by Mademoiselle' (8). But all is not quite as it seems: already there are hints that some order, some generative principle, some concept of family life is passing away. 'There were no words for it, of course, and the sense of it came only intermittently. Looking back now, one might express it by saying that there seemed disillusionments lurking, unformulated doubts about overcoming difficulties; a defeat somewhere, a failure of the vital impulse' (15).

This paragraph follows directly on a description of the children's now-dead grandmother – 'passionate spirit, loving and loved; modest, self-confident; sheltered, sharply independent; despotic matriarch, young girl pliant and caressing;

fragility, energy with a core like the crack and sting of a whip' (15). Our attention is being firmly directed towards a past generation and towards its links with the present. And yet a couple of pages later we learn from Mrs Jardine's own lips that she has *bought* the painting of her daughter that hangs in her bedroom, and that she has never (at that point) seen her grandchildren. The confidence is calculated and effective; 'some sort of conspiracy' (17) is being entered into.

The story shifts to 'a few months later', when Rebecca and her sister meet the famous, unknown grandchildren, Maisie, Malcolm and Charity ('Cherry'); other meetings follow. The children become friends; in particular Maisie, with her yearning, exasperated love for Cherry and her passionate jealous enmity of Mrs Jardine, becomes 'the first woman friend I ever had' (46). Maisie is not, of course, adult; she is only a few years older than Rebecca; but the exigencies of the story demand that she communicate to Rebecca information about her mother's (Ianthe's) desertion that can only be conveyed in long descriptive conversations untypical of schoolgirls. She shows Rebecca a miniature of Ianthe – 'She was Mrs Darling. She was a French New Year card angel-face, set in tinsel and blossoms. She was every child's dream of a beautiful mother' (52). Dream-mother, absent-mother. What is being described here is the relatively recent past, of Maisie's own childhood.

The next section belongs to Tilly, and the Chinese-box effect of her story-within-a-story; we are further back in the past now; the events related must belong to thirty or forty years earlier. We hear what Tilly has gleaned from the Landon grandmother about Sibyl Jardine's first marriage, her flight from it with a lover, and her husband's refusal afterwards to let her see Ianthe. Sibyl attempts a child snatch – much vivid quoted conversation here from servants, which one must suppose to have been recounted verbatim by Sibyl to her friend and thence to Tilly herself. The snatch is foiled; Sibyl is subsequently abandoned by her lover in the best Victorian tradition, and becomes an outcast from polite society. Some years later she reappears in London:

'Ah dear!' said Tilly. 'Pore Miss Sibyl! She's seen the seamy side alright. Toured all over the world in low-class theatrical companies, she 'ad – if she was to be believed; and writin' things for the newspapers, and I don't know what. As a girl, she was always one to go on about women's rights – and they should all be trained up to perfessions like men, and be the equal of them. Equals! she got her bellyful all right [. . .]' (89).

It is on the strength of such very occasional passages that *The Ballad and the Source* has been claimed as a 'feminist' work. The claim does not seem to me to stand up to the most cursory examination. Sibyl Jardine is, on the contrary, the prototype of female strengths and weaknesses: emotion-ruled yet manipulative, scheming, constantly attempting to get her way by making use of others and by arrogating to herself the rôle of victim. It is impossible to imagine her leading any kind of genuinely independent or emancipated life. By Tilly's account she attempts to use Rebecca's grandmother to effect a reunion with Ianthe, an attempt which is again foiled. Later, getting her own back, she writes an inflammatory novel – '"It was about a woman what was wronged all right," said Tilly with dramatic scorn. "Wronged by men. Wronged by a woman she trusted, one 'oo turned out a false friend and stabbed 'er to the 'eart"' (91). It is after this that the estrangement takes place between her and Rebecca's grandmother.

There is, however, a theme of female suffering more obliquely indicated in Tilly's saga which seems more central to the book's message. The wrong done by an ill-matched Victorian marriage has been the source of all subsequent disaster. Tilly's description of Sibyl Jardine's first husband is a piece of vintage Jamesian dialogue, in that it is incomprehensible to the listener (Rebecca) but not to the adult reader:

' "Of course (. . .) 'e was a sober sort of gentleman. Methodi-
cal. All books, books, books, and fiddle, fiddle with 'is precious
china, and tinkle, tinkle, tinkle on the 'arpsichord. Not like a
real man – for all 'e was a 'andsome well-set-up sort of feller
. . . 'He's never cared for female society, you know, Tilly,' she
says. 'He says women don't understand ideas' " ' (62).

The point is made still more clearly a page later:

[. . .] 'What she wanted was a flesh and blood man to govern 'er.
Break 'er and make 'er. Mark my words, 'e was better furnished in
the top storey than 'e was elsewhere, was that joker.'
A convulsion of laughter seized Tilly. Aware of its lewdness, I
wrestled fruitlessly to attach nameless implications to a whirling
composite picture of wardrobes, chairs, tables, beds, and, at the
very tip-top of a perpendicular staircase, one well-set-up gentleman
tinkling with china fingers on the harpsichord' (64).

Sexual fulfilment, failed or achieved, and at what cost,
haunts this book, though other themes – lying, truth etc. – are
less convincingly and more insistently offered. There is, for
instance, the moment early on when Rebecca sees Harry
Jardine carry his invalidish wife into the house. The sight
brings Rebecca 'one of those intimations, or premonitions,
which visit children, of a whole range of complex personal
emotions, far ahead of their present capacity, alien to their
experience, yet recognised in a prophetic flash as theirs to
come. What love would be like' (34). Later in the novel, the
same image is re-created between Mrs Jardine and the sculptor,
Gil.

Section Three, still set in the same pre-war summer, opens
with the death of Maisie, Malcolm and Cherry's absent father,
a circumstance that suits Mrs Jardine very well. She makes
divide-and-possess plans for her grandchildren, which include
the idea that she and Harry will carry Cherry off to a house
they own in the south of France. In the course of a monumen-

tally long conversation she holds with Rebecca, the past time is shifted rather nearer: we are approaching the present, as it were, by another route. We learn that Ianthe had an earlier child before the three living ones: '"He died. He was denied his life. My eldest grandson"' (107). She also describes, in impressionist, allusive terms, the growing Ianthe's relationship with her father, which seems to have been emotionally, if not physically, incestuous: '"He taught her that the natural love between a man and a woman, the love that makes them wish to live together and have children, was loathsome and degrading"' (125). Then she recounts how Ianthe and her father lived in Florence together, how he died, and how she was entrusted to the dubious care of a clergyman and his wife. Mrs Jardine travelled to Florence, re-met her daughter at last, and was not impressed. Subsequently she sent her own lover Paul (this again is clearer to the reader than to Rebecca) to Florence, hoping to make Ianthe fall in love with him and thus be improved by suffering. (What a long way from the Demeter myth we are here, to be sure!) However – as the reader is surely meant to foresee – Paul and Ianthe fall in love mutually and make off together. Ianthe, equally predictably, is later abandoned by Paul and, with Tilly's help, gives birth to her stillborn son in a small village in Bohemia: '"That beautiful child had been denied his life, Paul's child. He would have been glorious"' (169). But Paul too is soon dead: apparently Ianthe attacked him: '"I heard that when he died – he died far away, alone in a hotel bedroom – he had on his forehead, above one temple, a horrible scar. He had no scar upon his beautiful brows in the days when we were together"' (168). Some time after that Ianthe has married ('a respectable middle-aged man' – i.e. not a proper lover in Lehmann-land) had her three children and abandoned them, apparently for sexual reasons – the pattern established in one generation working itself out in the next. This section ends with Mrs

Jardine telling Rebecca that she does not have 'the slightest idea' where Ianthe is now (175).

Section Four introduces Auntie Mack, the children's spinster cousin, to fill in further details and to tell Rebecca that in fact Ianthe did not go off with a man but deserted her children because of some more fundamental instability and failure of feeling. The recital of the past has now caught up with the present, and in Section Five time begins to move on: autumn is coming, Tilly is dead, the grandchildren are leaving the house on the hill. Mrs Jardine and Harry go to France, taking Cherry with them, leaving Maisie and Malcolm at schools. Letters arrive with news of Cherry's health and happiness and of the very special governess, Tanya Moore, who has been 'picked' (Mrs Jardine's usual inflated terminology) to take care of her. Then, the following March, Cherry suddenly dies. By and by a long, genuinely agonised letter arrives from Mrs Jardine:

'I thought I could save her, my lamb, my own flesh and blood – and I could not. The virtue has gone out of me, I suppose. Nothing has been spared me, nothing. I am mocked by day and by night. An old, barren woman. Must I be *taught to die*, while I still draw breath, that I am thrust again, again – and now *irrevocably* – into this pit where all experience is proof of *nothing* – *no* warmth, *no* light, *no* colour, *no* happiness, *no love*? Like a wounded snake I drag my slow length along [. . .]' (210).

Not for another thirteen years was Rosamond Lehmann to experience such a loss herself. Then she too, as she puts it in *The Swan in the Evening*, 'had to learn, and re-learn, and learn again day after day, week after week, month after month, that I was truly left behind to crawl on as best I could, eternal exile, through the stone streets full of other people's daughters' (118).

Cherry's death – off-stage, appropriately, in a book where all the significant events are off-stage – is the climax of the novel. After that, its tension deteriorates, and the final third of the book is the weakest, the most diffuse and the part where one is most aware of the creaking of the structure. A year passes; there is further news from France, the sculptor Gil has appeared on the scene there. Then the all-significant outbreak of the 1914 war comes. Life in the Landon home diminishes, becomes sadder. Then, in 1916, the lumpy Malcolm reappears, in the slightly improbable guise of a charming young man off to the Front. (Before the end of the novel he will, of course, be killed. Jess, Rebecca's sister, to whom he has been writing, has his letters and a photograph: 'not very like anybody in particular: mass-produced photograph of a dead English subaltern', 316.) Meanwhile both the past and the present in the novel are substantially moved on by a dinner party held in the winter of 1916 in the house on the hill by Maisie, Malcolm, Tanya Moore – who is now out of favour in France because she has seduced Gil away from Mrs Jardine – and Gil himself. It is some sort of *rite de passage*, marking the child characters' transition to adulthood, and the romantic lovers are now Tanya and Gil, who are getting married. During the evening Maisie recounts to Rebecca the final story in the Ianthe saga – how she turned up in France, mad,* in 1914, and the scene that ensued with Gil's stone heads – an ultimate, five-part power struggle between Ianthe, Mrs Jardine, Gil, Tanya and Maisie herself, in a hyper-romantic setting that detracts from, rather than adding to, the story's impact. We have met trees and water very often before in Rosamond Lehmann's work, and they tend to accompany, not events of lasting significance, but an ephemeral drama.

---

* As a footnote to this theme, which does not seem to be properly worked out in *The Ballad and the Source*, I record the fact that Rosamond Lehmann's youngest sister, the actress Beatrix Lehmann, had published in 1934 a novel called *Rumour of Heaven* (Methuen), in which a mother goes mad and deserts her children.

Tanya never comes to life as a character; nor, much, does Gil – but he at least is given a memorable line when he unexpectedly kisses Rebecca (who must then be about fifteen). '"I know you're a well-brought up, well-educated English girl," he said. "But all the same, you seem so nice and dark"' (245).

It is that darkness – that mysterious sexuality – that is at the heart of Rosamond Lehmann's heroines, and of her novels too, and which redeems into intensity much that, when re-counted baldly, may sound hyper-romantic, far-fetched or even novelettish.

CHAPTER IX

Waters

When Rosamond Lehmann published *The Ballad and the Source* in 1944, she was writing of a period thirty years earlier. When she came to publish *A Sea-Grape Tree* in 1976 – the short novel that has the adult Rebecca as its central protagonist – she was writing of a time over forty years earlier, and 'the war' is, yet again, the First World War. Just as when *The Ballad and the Source* came out, critics made reference to *A Sea-Grape Tree*'s lack of relevance to the present day: I do not propose to answer those criticisms: 'relevance' is, arguably, not the standard by which such a poetic work, so concerned with vision, should be judged. Rosamond Lehmann herself regards it as an experimental work, dealing in an original way with time and place, and was disappointed by its reception. But I think it fair to say that, if she failed to get across in it the spiritual and imaginative message she hoped to convey, that is partly because readers found that the period setting, and the full-blown romanticism of the love-story that the novel tells detracted from the reality it might otherwise have had.

It was, however, impossible that the novel should be other than a period piece, since one of the impulses behind its creation was the author's desire to explore how Sibyl Jardine, of *The Ballad and the Source*, ended her days. The fact that Mrs Jardine is dead before the novel opens does not affect this aim, since she appears at length to Rebecca (now tiresomely calling herself 'Anonyma') in what seems to be a waking dream. Rosamond Lehmann's belief that the dead continue an existence elsewhere, and can be contacted by the living, has informed her life since the death of Sally in 1958, and inevitably informs this late novel also. Examination of such a belief is outside the scope of this study. But I think most literary critics would agree that it does not seem to work well as a component of a novel, perhaps mainly because novels are essentially about people inter-reacting in this world rather than contemplating the next: the introduction of mystic perceptions seems to pre-empt this world of the importance it must have, if the novel is to convince and involve the reader.

It is true that an interest in, for instance, extra-sensory perception, is occasionally apparent in the novels long before such interests surfaced in Rosamond Lehmann's own life: her conviction could hardly have sprung, new born, without psychological antecedents. One may feel that fleeting moments of such visionary insight – as when Olivia, in *The Weather in the Streets*, guesses that Nicola is pregnant – work better than a fully formulated belief system. In any case every novel, including one with mystic, allegoric or science-fiction elements, needs to create its own internal reality on a coherent level: in *A Sea-Grape Tree*, however, the mode of reality to which we are being asked to accommodate varies considerably from one part to another – something which was already a problem, though to a lesser extent, with *The Ballad and the Source*. In some ways the story elements of the late novel are quintessential Lehmann, fixed forever somewhere around the date of *The Weather in the Streets*, and certain passages have the familiar authenticity, truth and sureness of touch but belong very much to *this* world in which there are no visionary comforts. It is set – like the play *No More Music* – on a Caribbean island, and, as I have already commented (see Chapter VII), some of that play's material re-surfaces. There is the boarding-house with its heterogeneous company, the soft-footed black servants, the sense of the island's personality – the spirit of the place. Rebecca-Anonyma has come there alone: she expected to be accompanied by her lover, but at the last moment he has deserted her, perhaps finally; she is in a bad state, Lehmann-woman at her most desperate and helpless with the unresolved sister–rivalries of childhood catching up with her once again, a background and chorus to her life –

'I used to think the main thing in everybody's life was love. But it isn't: I found that out long ago. People can manage with only a pinch of it – if that. They're not nice people but they function. I literally can't. I *cannot* live without love: without – you know, being in a state of love [. . .]' (125–6).

'. . . The mere sight of me would utterly dismay [my mother]. Trouble, trouble, she would guess. Were I to break down and tell her, she would give dreadful good advice. Strange but true, families are the cruellest company in these predicaments: forcing you back to the roots, and oh! how the roots tug, threaten, ache; whispering the old competitive comparisons, guilts, atavisms, insecurities. Plain, pretty; clever, stupid; naughty, good; bad marks, top marks; spiteful; selfish; jealous; unfair; unkind; unjust; your fault; my fault; his fault; her fault; best loved, not loved, lonely, lonely, lonely, failure, FAILURE . . .' (85).

'"I like unpleasant characters,"' Rebecca also confides, and her listener replies '". . . I'm afraid you do. Something tells me that's your trouble"' (75).

The betraying lover figures only as quintessential betraying male. ('They all let her down in the end', as someone says in the same book, of Mrs Jardine.) Not till Rebecca has found other arms to shelter her do we hear any details about him. He is married, with children; a freelance journalist of whose activities she is never entirely sure: sometimes, she admits, she has wondered if he is working in Intelligence.

'A spy, you think he might be.'
'Some sort. It would fit in with something in his character that mystifies me: his way of looking you particularly straight in the eye, and at the same time making a sort of complicated – verbal – sidestep

which only strikes you as odd when you think about it afterwards [. . .] He always swore – I really thought he meant it.'

'Meant what?'

'That he couldn't do without me. He's a very brilliant man – and attractive – and the opposite of dull. When we first met he was pretty well the top, non-queer, slightly disreputable glamour-boy in circulation. Perhaps you don't realise how scarce they are on the ground these days. Girls have to look around . . .' (130).

One is irresistibly reminded of the betraying lover, Jocelyn, in *The Echoing Grove*, who swore to Madeleine that she was the most important person for him and finally, when accosted by her after deserting her, '"[. . .] kept on looking in the glass, so I knew it was Jocelyn. It's one of his habits. As if he was watching himself and wondering who he was"' (290. See Chapter x). Innumerable 'spotters' have annoyed Rosamond Lehmann by assuming this character in *The Echoing Grove* to be Cecil Day Lewis. If it 'was' anybody, she says, it was someone much further back in time. I think that *A Sea-Grape Tree* tends to reinforce this. But the point is, once again, that the false lover who is such a constant figure in Lehmann-land is there long before the author ever met Cecil Day Lewis, Goronwy Rees or anyone else: he appears brutally in *Dusty Answer* (Roddy), more benignly as Hugh in *A Note in Music*, and as Tony Heriot, with whom Kate falls in love in *Invitation to the Waltz*.

A Sea-Grape Tree also features those other Lehmann-land inhabitants, the wonderful young man and the soldier damaged in the war: here they are conflated into one person, Johnny, who rescues Rebecca from grief at desertion. He is presented as a paraplegic who can swim but not walk, and who spends most of his days in a hut on the beach attended by a faithful native. He is married, like Timmy the blind man in *Invitation to the Waltz*, to a nurse of a different social class from his own, but – and here the author's fantasy and prejudice take over, for nurses are always dislikable in her books! — she neglects him. Rebecca comforts him, as he does her: she gives him back the gift of virility; in spite of paralysis from the waist down they make love successfully. (The relationship with the nurse has, he tells her, been a *mariage blanc*). The improbability of this new-found virility, the lack of any reference to the other inconveniences of paraplegia, in short the very strong element of day-dream, seems a considerable debasement of the standards of authenticity hitherto prevailing in Lehmann-land. One can only conclude that the whole episode is meant to be something in the nature of a restorative dream, sufficient unto itself. Indeed, to do the author justice, although there is talk of a life together and a hoped for baby, in the closing pages, it is not at all clear that, once Rebecca has left the island, she will see Johnny again either. The message of the book seems to be, rather, that whatever trials and betrayals people suffer, in the words of the spectral Mrs Jardine: '"Nothing is lost, Rebecca, nothing of love is lost"' (79).

Mrs Jardine, widowed, came to the island some years before, there fell in love with Johnny herself, and died; Rebecca sees a photo of her grave. Johnny is there because it is a refuge for him in his damaged state; Rebecca too finds it a refuge and perhaps a means of facing life again. To the owners, inhabitants and hangers-on of the boarding-house — including Miss Stay, who is clairvoyant but otherwise resembles Auntie Mack in *The Ballad and the Source* — it is the place of a retreat from a post-war life with which, for varying reasons, they cannot cope.

One competent, coping character whose life is continuing to happen and move *does* appear — but only in a fantasy of Rebecca's. It is Maisie, Mrs Jardine's granddaughter. Apparently she was summoned to the island when Mrs Jardine became frail, and remained there till the old lady's death. She has become a doctor, in spite of a childhood fear of blood —

a neat and convincing piece of evolution. Rebecca is shown a photograph of her with a small child in her arms; Maisie has kept to her vow never to marry, but she has not been afraid to bear a child: she has achieved what Mrs Jardine and Ianthe (not to mention Olivia in *The Weather in the Streets*) were insufficiently independent in any sense to do. Rebecca imagines a conversation in which Maisie is very much the robust, professional woman of the world: she (Rebecca) stammers out a half-formed ambition to become a doctor, but Maisie pooh-poohs this, telling Rebecca how unsuited she would be to the life. Instead she invites her to stay and help care for the child, a small, fierce girl who has the promise of beauty: Mrs Jardine's one descendant and vindication for existence.

This fantasy within a fantasy acquires an extra dimension of significance when one knows that Rosamond Lehmann herself, circa 1940, feeling that her life was a failure, toyed with the idea of starting over again and training in medicine: 'I did actually go and see the head of the Oxford Medical School – he thought I wasn't at all suitable, that I'd never stand it – and when I told Cecil (Day Lewis) I was thinking of giving up writing, he said "You're mad! You're a very good writer! You're a born writer!"' (Janet Watts, *Harper's & Queen*, 1982).

One must agree that Cecil Day Lewis was right.

Rebecca is another of those vaguely worrying writer's *alter egos* that are minus the essential creativity that makes the writer what she is. Like Olivia, like Dinah in *The Echoing Grove*, she has evolved for herself only a sub-artistic, sub-literary existence – '"I've worked in a bookshop, and a decorating shop –"' (62). No wonder, the reader feels, that by the time she reaches the island, with its pervasive suggestion of Prospero's magic isle with healing powers, she is badly in need of such succour – indeed, almost suicidal:

The island is one of the smallest of the Windward Islands, not at all fashionable. Up to this year, which is 1933, it has scarcely begun to emerge from a paradisal state. Birds, butterflies, flowers, shrubs, flowering trees, and creepers abound in immeasurable splendour, profusion and variety. No snakes. Idyllic isle. Only the natives do not correspond (7).

The theme of this last remark is not pursued: it is almost as if it has crept in from some other story which Rosamond Lehmann thought of writing but from which she got deflected. The island has both a personal and a literary antecedent for her: the Isle of Wight, the place of idyllic childhood summers, that figures as such in 'The Red-haired Miss Daintreys' (see Chapter VII) is one of the key places mentioned in *The Swan in the Evening* as part of the essential landscape of childhood:

The Isle is supposed to eject those whom it does not fancy. Be that as it may, it went on harbouring us, year after year, and indeed generation after generation. My mother brought my father, in a bath chair, to be benefited (was he?) by the mild sea air, for as long as journeys were possible at all. Helen and I both came as young married women, with our children. Later we came back, each one of us, in a more solitary and occasional way . . .

Rosamond Lehmann goes on to describe how she eventually bought a plot of land on the island 'after my mother's death' and had built on it a small house, which she had intended as 'a sort of Wedding present for my daughter Sally: somewhere, if she and Patrick went on living abroad, as seemed likely, they could return to; a refuge always waiting for their children. She was pleased at the prospect, but she never saw it' (77). On her marriage to Patrick Kavanagh, Sally accompanied him to Java, where he was working as a British Council lecturer, and there she died suddenly of poliomyelitis the following year. Rosamond Lehmann was in fact in the small house on the island 'measuring for carpets and curtains', on that date: by one of those terrible ironies life sometimes inflicts, the place of safety became the place from which she returned only to hear that the one relationship of safety had been struck by death. By another coincidence – though some might argue that it was not a coincidence at all – that morning Rosamond Lehmann had found a dead bird on the terrace of the barely-completed house: it must have flown into the glass door without seeing it, and broken its neck. One remembers the dead bird that occupies something of the same symbolic role in *A Note in Music* (see Chapter 1) written thirty years before, and also the dead or wounded birds the child Rosamond had tried to save.

On a small island the sea is ever-present, and the beach itself is where much of *A Sea-Grape Tree*'s action takes place, a real sub-tropical beach with the sea-grape tree's 'glaucous blue-fleshed leaves and pendant clusters of green berries' (11) but also quintessential everywhere beach: 'A vast seashore flashed open suddenly: abstract of the loved, played-on shores of childhood, the tide far out, cobbles and shingle sloping to tawny sand with ripples on its surface, the light strange, sunless' (26). The sea itself is Johnny's healing element, and it is in his beach-hut that they make love. One recalls other shores, other seas which have played the same idyllic rôle in earlier novels. In *The Weather in the Streets* Olivia and Rollo visit a deserted Dorset beach, late in the afternoon on their first weekend away together: all is benign, pure, full of promise, troubles still locked away in the future. In *The Echoing Grove* Rickie and Dinah, after a far more equivocal and stormy relationship, escape together to a Welsh shore for what is intended to be a brief oasis in their separate lives. The rough water images which are frequent in this novel as a metaphor or analogue to emotional turmoil, temporarily coalesce with a real, calm sea. Dinah, convalescent from the stillborn birth of Rickie's child and a subsequent suicide attempt, has persuaded him: '"[. . .] If I could be by the sea, somewhere quiet, for a short time alone with you, I know I'd – be healed in no time. And after that you'll see – I'll be no trouble"' (126).

But their time away works its perilous magic:

They walked hand in hand, bathed, picnicked, prawned; in a few days they were tanned, salty, ravenous. Before the week was ended he was hopelessly in love with her again. [On their last night]: They were one, they could not live apart, they knew it. In the morning, before he left, they agreed upon their future course. He would await Madeleine's return, then at once, straightforwardly, tell her that his mind was made up, he was going away with Dinah. Where? Never mind that now. Some island on the other side of the world . . . (126–8).

But *The Echoing Grove* unlike *A Sea-Grape Tree*, is essentially concerned not with out-of-time dreams but with the going-on of time, and this carries Rickie and Dinah away from one another again, fatally and permanently. As another character – Georgie – later remarks, their idyll has not been 'life-like' (263). The 'abstract of the loved, played-on shores of childhood' offers, in adult life, no real substance. In 1951 Rosamond Lehmann herself wrote a poem* in which this truth is, by implication, faced:

> THE BAY
> Here the white strand again; no change;
> This gap in time revisited,
> The lucent dream, the cryptic shore,
> Moon, stars, transparencies once more:
> A cryptic dream, the same; and strange;
> Time past; time found again; time dead.
>
> Again these cliffs, this blinding arc
> Powdered and silvered, rock-embossed;
> That minatory reef whereon
> Our non-committal charts are lost,
> The revenant† leaps to save: the dark
> Spectre swings, falls, bleeds white, is gone.

*Typescript and manuscript copies in King's College Library, Cambridge.
†In handwritten original 'victim'.

Wave whispering, thin foam; and drift
Of palm-shell, coral, leaf, wood, bone;
Wind fret and fret or ripple; shift,
Silence; the moonfire-threaded mesh
Dredging the pools; and I alone,
Expecting no one, not expected;
Presence although of human flesh
Abstract as water, bare as stone,
Reflecting naught, and unreflected.

Yet on this verge I still behold
A weightless imprint, less than shade,
Starker than moon, as soft, as cold, –
Eternal ghost, forever laid –
Once, by a double image made.

RL. 1951.

If the sea shore is one of Rosamond Lehmann's 'powerful images', the river is another, more ubiquitous one in her work and one planted extremely early. R. C. Lehmann had been a champion oarsman: boating and swimming expeditions were part of the stuff of the Lehmanns' childhood. Both motifs – the sea and the river – flow through 'The Red-haired Miss Daintreys': the Ellisons meet the Daintreys on the Isle of Wight; later the Daintreys are invited to the Bourne End house, a social occasion which the children dimly and with consternation perceive to be awkward for their parents. It symbolises much else about the Daintreys that they are not water-creatures: even Viola, the second daughter, who looks like a French Impressionist painting of a siren with her red tresses, does not indulge: 'I am sure I should have remembered them in bathing suits. My belief is that none of them could swim. I know I got the notion that sea-water must be injurious to people of their complexion' (*The Gipsy's Baby*, 65). The later Thames swimming party is haunted by an unnamed sense of elegy, intimations of the loss of childhood innocence, disguised with an ironic humour:

This must be towards evening when it grew cooler, and Pa and Ma were conducted down to the boathouse to watch us swim. Ma said we were pretty dears; the sight of our bonny limbs seemed to cause her sorrow and foreboding ... She asked my mother whether she felt quite happy about the effects of immersion upon us in our overheated condition. She herself never trusted river water. The only son of a dear widowed cousin of hers had swallowed a fatal mouthful of bacteria while bathing. He was gone in a week (81).

Later in the story Miss Mildred Daintrey dies on the voyage to China and is buried at sea. With the deceptively unconcentrated air that is characteristic of this most subtle of all her works, the author remarks: 'Only the other night I re-read a volume of stories called *Rhapsody* by Dorothy Edwards and came upon these words: "There is something very attractive about the thought of the skeletons of red-haired people"; and I thought of the white bones of Miss Mildred picked by the currents of the Indian Ocean' (89).

Elsewhere in the novels river and lake scenes and bathing scenes are too numerous to mention individually; often they mark some sort of climax or resolution of the plot, as in *A Note in Music* where a swim in the lake for some members of the party is part of the idyllic day out in the country house garden (but Grace, significantly, won't swim) – or in *The Weather in the Streets* where Rollo, on a unique occasion, joins Olivia's other world of Anna, Simon and Colin in a swimming party near the cottage. In *The Ballad and the Source* the presence of the river – that French river with the weir and the inn that was one of the germs of the book – is central to the final episode in the saga of Ianthe: Maisie describes swimming in it in ecstatic terms that inevitably carry, for the analytically sophisticated reader, an additional message:

'I liked letting my legs go with the turn-over of the water till they almost began to feel dissolved, as if they were pouring over the edge too [. . .] Then I used to slip down and let myself go under into the plunge of the weir and come up again farther along with the drift of the current, and float – float into the calm stream again. Of course it was only a little tame weir, but gosh! it was heaven' (260).

In *Dusty Answer*, that novel of ubiquitous but unfocussed sexuality, the river is such a constant presence that the whole novel seems arranged along its banks. It is in a dream of river bathing that the dead Charlie re-appears, only to depart again:

He did not speak. He emerged swiftly from among them, and they all watched him in silence while he stooped to the dim river and slipped in. He turned his face, his hidden face, downstream, and went floating and swimming gently along. He too was happy.

A dark misty solitude of night and water was ahead of him, and he went into it without pause or backward look, and it folded around him. Horror crept in: for he was disappearing (47).

Immediately, on the next page which opens Part II, Judith is really swimming in the river at night, on her own, enjoying the biting chill, watching the now-adult children-next-door who have just returned to the house. By this same river at night after a boating expedition, Roddy will make love to her. And it is in another but similar river that Judith and Jennifer swim naked, and indulge in the sort of emotional adoration of one another that has made a more worldly-wise generation refer to these passages as the 'lesbian love interest'. Not all the bathing in this book is benign, though. In the south of France Judith and Julian swim in a pool; he is nearly carried over a waterfall and hauls himself back with his legs and arms grazed and bleeding: tormented Julian is not a natural swimmer. And it is in this book that the Isle of Wight, the magic isle, and its sea turn vengeful, for Martin, unfulfilled lover, gallant loser, archetype of all those decent young men destroyed in the war, is drowned yachting off its shores.

Finally, in *The Echoing Grove*, a metaphor of diving into deep water surfaces in Rickie's long conversation with Georgie before his death; it seems to embody the concepts of emotional and sexual 'letting go' *and* that of launching the spirit into another element: death, madness — or something more? The living Rickie does not know. And the dead one cannot — in this book — tell us.

Weather has also been an important ingredient in Rosamond Lehmann's writing, a way by which feeling is heightened and paralleled. Sometimes the device is that of the straight pathetic fallacy, awarding to individual emotion a universal dimension — as in *Dusty Answer*:

She cried aloud and woke into a night streaming, blind with the rain's enormous weeping.
He never came again.
His son was born and his grandmother died; but he was too far, too spent a ghost to raise his head at that (47).

Sometimes, as in the short stories, extremes of weather are used as a more sophisticated metaphor for personal traumas (See Chapter VII). More simply, in *A Note in Music* and *Invitation to the Waltz*, both Grace Fairfax and Olivia Curtis are highly aware of nature and the seasons around them, but in both of them this seems partly the result of their relative *emptiness* — their expectancy of something that does not come to pass but which, at any rate for Olivia, might in the future. *Invitation to the Waltz* ends, indeed, on a note of adolescent pantheism and innocent excitement:

Everything's going to begin. A hare sitting up in the grass took fright, darting ahead of her into the ploughed land. The rooks flew up in a swirl from the furrows. All the landscape as far as the horizon seemed to begin to move. Wind was chasing cloud, and sun flew behind them. A winged gigantic runner with a torch was running from a great distance to meet her, swooping over the low hills, skimming from them veil after veil of shadow, touching them to instant ethereal shapes of light. On it came, over ploughed field and fallow. The rooks flashed sharply, the hare and his shadow swerved in sudden sunlight. In a moment it would be everywhere. Here it was. She ran into it (301–2).

In *A Note in Music*, which takes place in the course of one calendar year, more or less, the sense of the changing seasons is more integrated with the process of what seems almost too slight a chain of events to be called a story, and yet at the same time Grace's passionate response to the weather has something pathological in it, a sign of her own frailness. She hates, fears and resents the cold northern winter and belated spring: in contrast, on her solitary holiday in the south, she 'falls into a summer trance'. Climate and landscape assume a disproportionate importance and power in a life so essentially low-key. But the obtrusiveness of the seasons indicating the passage of time is particularly interesting in a novel in which time itself – or rather, the absence of time – is a theme. Grace in particular feels that she has nothing much to show for the years she has lived, and will never have anything more: so, to a dimmer extent, does Tom. Norah has had certain things happen to her, but that was in the past. None of the characters, including Hugh to whom things *do* appear to 'happen', looks forward to anything. When the novel ends, Grace has bidden goodbye to Hugh, telling herself and him '"As long as I'm alive I shall think of you somewhere in the world, still gay and lucky . . . So you must promise me you'll be so always"' (243). This small, selfless perception is, it seems, to sustain her emotionally for the rest of her days. The book's title, at first sight suitable for a record of fleeting moments, is revealed, on closer examination, as running counter to the theme. It is taken from a line of Walter Savage Landor, 'But the present, like a note in music, is nothing but as it appertains to what is past and what is to come.' In fact, in this novel, the present is *all* that exists, and has to be sufficient unto itself. In the closing pages Grace finds no other refuge but 'thinking cosmically': 'If one could [. . .] keep one's mind strained to it even for one minute without collapsing – then one would be brushed by a fleeting intimation of what life was' (308-9). But such reflections lead only, as they must, into a void in which love itself becomes meaningless, obsolete:

[. . .] He would die in his own time; someone would wash him, fold his hands, arrange his funeral. Hugh would have a funeral, a burial service, wreaths . . . in his coffin, his body would fall into corruption . . . and someone would be busy in his room, sorting his clothes, putting away his pipes, his books, reading and burning his old letters . . .
And that was that (311).

Not till she came to write that supremely accomplished work *The Echoing Grove* was Rosamond Lehmann able to achieve the trick of making both the immediacies of love *and* the long inevitabilities of time agonizingly real, in a novel whose weaving time-scheme is a *tour de force* of psychological truth:

And so all these years later, in another room in another house of his, vacated by him in perpetuity, lying awaiting no one in the bed, the same, in which she had once lain to be taken by him, bodilessly penetrated through darkness and in separation at a given time by the long-awaited breaking of his silence, Dinah now turned away from him, rejecting – she could, she was still alive – his wistful thoughts of her; breaking resolutely – she must, life must go on – from the trap of his pursuing shadow (145).

The Weather in the Streets, like *A Note in Music*, also covers a year's cycle – slightly more – and, as the title itself suggests, the growth, fruition and disintegration of Olivia and Rollo's relationship is both determined in practical terms, and orchestrated in emotional ones, by the changing seasons. Their affair germinates as a winter thing, secret, sheltered from the storm – 'indoors or in taxis or in his warm car [. . .] Drawn curtains, shaded lamp, or only the fire . . .' (145). It is still winter when they manage their first weekend away together, but 'The air was like April. It smelt of primroses, I said' (169). In the spring, loving passionately, Olivia falls ill, a symbolic fever:

in May and June Rollo is away in America and she is in the country. Rollo returns, there is an idyllic day – and then, under the sun of an Austrian summer, they achieve their time of splendour. From then on decline begins; in August, the 'sinister pause in the year', Olivia is pregnant in the 'dry, sterile, burnt out end of summer' (263). Rollo is absent again. Once her calvary is over, the autumn has set in. Together they revisit the country but it is damp and drear, the magic has departed – 'the transfiguring light was gone, and it was dark and cold now, blowing up for rain' (330). The story ends amid the sleet and fog of winter, with Simon dead, Rollo incapacitated and reclaimed by his own family. Yet he will recover, he speaks enticingly of the future: spring will return. The reader strongly suspects that this is *not* in fact the end of the story. In this novel indeed nature and human nature are in perfect literary synthesis.

CHAPTER X

The infernal grove

In a broadcast she gave at the time *The Echoing Grove* came out in 1953 Rosamond Lehmann said that, as she had been

tunnelling to find a way through to the end of it, I began to feel that, more than any of the others, this novel had something to do with the first I ever wrote [*Dusty Answer*]. Not the same one in a fresh guise; not even a development from it; but more as if somehow – I cannot explain why – some cycle of experience that had opened when I was a girl was now coming to a close.

It is possible to see *The Echoing Grove* itself in terms of a 'cycle of experience' – the elaborate time-scheme employed in it, and the way events in it repeat themselves, with modifications, suggest a circularity of time. But for the moment I should like to consider Rosamond Lehmann's remark in more concrete terms, applied as it is to her own life and the experiences which became the stuff of her fiction. With Judith in *Dusty Answer*, Lehmann-woman began her passionate exploration – passionate in every sense. Where, by the time of *The Echoing Grove*, has this exploration carried her? What answer had she found? Indeed, a dusty one. For *The Echoing Grove*, though masterly as a novel and as an evocation of feeling and time-lived, cannot be said to present an optimistic view of life. The themes of betrayal, of loss, of the loved person as a chimera who must ultimately escape the lover, – themes that were there in the first novel, are here in the last major one, reinforced and turned implacably into the central theme. It is not a book for the young who are still inventing their lives, but for the middle-aged, to whom experience has become a

palimpsest with recurrent patterns. A woman of my acquaintance, whose own life-patterns have been far more fortunate
than Rosamond Lehmann's, has said that nevertheless she
finds *The Echoing Grove* so sad she can hardly bear to read
it. What effect its terrible honesty must have on readers who
are themselves in the grip of destructive patterns, one can
hardly bear to think.

An American critic, writing of Rosamond Lehmann in the
last ten years, when her value and importance has gradually
begun to be recognised again on both sides of the Atlantic,
has described the central defeat suffered by Lehmann-woman
thus:

'Invariably human sexuality is the principal means for an attempt to
impose the self upon experience, to create an intense connection that
can assuage the inevitable forces of time, history, death . . . The sense
of sexual connection, of expressing the self in a close relationship, is
more important than the nature of the relationship's object.'

It is however in consequence of this, he seems to imply, that

'In all the novels the sexual connections are transitory, defeated, the
heroines left alone at the end with the recognition that they have
nothing beyond themselves' (James Gindin, 'Rosamond Lehmann: a
Revaluation', *Wisconsin Studies in Contemporary Literature*, Vol.
15, 1974).

In *The Echoing Grove* the basic elements we have met
before in the other novels and stories are all present: the
relationship between sisters – now with its tension fully revealed at last, the mother-figure as a strong point of sense
and continuity, the wicked mother-in-law, the sick, dead or
otherwise absent father-figure (two), the young men killed in
war (now the Second World War), the dead child (in more
than one form), the juxtaposition of a Bohemian with a more
conventional and monied life-style. There is also the wonderful
young man figure, now rather older but still loved and admired

by all, still coming from a grand if now financially depleted background, still in some sense elusive. There is desperate, corrosive jealousy (Madeleine), loneliness and social dislocation (Dinah), and, most centrally and inescapably, there is betrayal, displayed as in a casebook in two forms: the endemic, chronic betrayal that follows on irreconcilable commitments, and which we met before in Rollo, is here demonstrated, far more terribly, in Rickie; as if this were not enough, the pain of acute betrayal is also there, when Madeleine finds herself abruptly left by her lover, Jocelyn.

As I say, all familiar elements. But they are presented in this final novel of the cycle in a particularly heightened and concentrated form. For the two sisters are also sexual rivals; the husband of one is lover to the other; the inbred jealousies of childhood, the 'roots that tug, threaten, ache', unite with the dreadful pangs of sexual possessiveness in a fight almost to the death. The worst betrayal of all is the perfidy of one sister towards another – the violation of a fundamental taboo, assaulting the very structure of the family. Indeed the author has remarked to me that, in her view, this novel is more about sisters than anything else, and even if one does not entirely agree with this assessment, there can be no mistaking the force of long-term emotion that is present.

Moreover the whole business, which has covered many years of the characters' lives, is viewed essentially in retrospect; there is hardly one moment, throughout the book, when we see love existentially, simply happening – what we are shown are its agonising, long-term consequences. This, indeed, is not the 'love that is warm, a meeting place', but love lost, denied, abandoned, destroyed, 'the suicide's grave under the nettles' (*Departure in the Dark*, Cecil Day Lewis). We know almost from the first page, before we know anything else of the story, that it has ended sadly, that there has been no victory for anyone, that Madeleine and Dinah are, at best, battered survivors. The suspense of the novel lies not in 'what next?' but in 'how?'

> They were meeting to be reconciled after fifteen years. This present mood in which they sat relaxed was nothing more than the relief of two people coming back to a bombed building once familiar, shared as a dwelling, and finding all over the smashed foundations a rose-ash haze of willow-herb. No more, no less. It is a ruin [. . .) an area razed, roped off by time [. . .] (13).

The precise visual image is right in more than one sense. Images of churned up, disturbed or re-sown earth, or buried objects, abound in this novel, but this particular picture of the horror-struck past as a blitzed building over which wild flowers have now grown points not only to the theme of destruction in the book but also to that of resolution. I have already commented in discussing Rosamond Lehmann's short stories (see Chapter VII) that whereas the First World War figures in her books as something casting a long shadow over people's lives, the Second is seen almost as a relief and an expiation, a final breaking of a spell. The war is not a 'bad' element in *The Echoing Grove*, for all that two characters die directly from it, one of them Rickie and Madeleine's eldest son, and that Rickie himself dies in its course. It finally changes everything, life-styles and relationships included, breaking a remorseless pattern, and it is only afterwards that Madeleine and Dinah can be reconciled. Not for nothing does the longest and most important scene in the book – if perhaps the oddest – the one between Rickie and Georgie, take place one night in the blitz.

Rosamond Lehmann has said that, after *The Echoing Grove*, she knew that she could never again write that kind of novel. One may take this remark as a comment on the novel's essential bleakness, the way it exposes love, the fruitful material of all the other novels, as a snare and a delusion, an 'infernal grove' to be 'rooted up'. Obviously, after that, a cycle *was* complete; Rosamond Lehmann could contribute nothing more to that particular territory. But one may also take the remark as a comment of a more benign and even optimistic nature, a comment on that resolution through time, and even salvation, that the book half promises. It is rather a low-key, bleak promise in itself, but it is nevertheless there: Madeleine, desperate at the loss of her lover, confides at last in Dinah, for so long her arch-rival. Dinah herself, once briefly married to a loving man who has been killed in the Spanish Civil War, has had to come to terms with much loss herself.

Madeleine asks her:

'Have you got anybody – '
   'A lover? No. Nor want. It's all over, it won't happen any more. I like company and I've got a few friends. I don't miss having an emotional life.'
   'It must be peaceful.'
   The words, an extinguished heart-wrung cry, brought Dinah's eyes to rest on her again; to watch her fumble in her handbag, extract a small handkerchief and dab her cheeks. Presently she said weeping:
   'Well, I shall not be saved.'
   'Madeleine, you will be. You are saved. It may not make sense to you just now, but I know it is so' (286–7).

Rosamond Lehmann has said to me: 'I find at my age I can hardly believe – imagine – that sex was once so important . . . All that business of being attracted to people and worrying about it and them . . .' The reflection seems to fit well with Dinah's quietest viewpoint, but the operative phrase is 'at my age': Rosamond was over eighty when she said that. One feels, when reading *The Echoing Grove*, that in the first and the last scenes Madeleine and Dinah are, if not exactly old, at any rate well advanced in middle age; they make elderly remarks ('My legs . . . Not that it matters tuppence', 14). It comes as a shock to realise, working the story out chronologically, that in 1946 (which is when the present of the book is situated) Madeleine is only forty-two and Dinah probably therefore forty at the most: rather young, one would say, for either woman to feel that physical and emotional love are over and done with.

We are dealing here, I would suggest, with chronological and psychological time which do not entirely coincide. On one level, the time-scheme of *The Echoing Grove* is very carefully worked out; dates are indicated, events in the characters' personal lives synchronise accurately with public events – the hard winter of 1931 (when Dinah bears her stillborn child), the outbreak of war, the battle of Tobruk (in which the son Anthony is killed), the battle of Narvik in which Dinah's friend Rob is killed. But on a more general time-scale something is amiss; the cumulative events of Rickie, Madeleine and Dinah's joint, intermingled lives seem to cover a larger span than is allotted to them – ('unfaithful at last to Dinah after all these years' thinks Rickie in the early 1930s on a trip abroad – 118). In fact, only two or three years can have elapsed since their affair began. Moreover, even on the practical plane of dates, the chronology is very tight. One commentator, noticing this, has made a terrier attempt to pin the subject down into one scheme and to reconcile the flaws:

If Rickie Masters was born in 1902 (which seems reasonable since he was twelve when his father died in 1914), and he married, as Mrs Burkett – his mother-in-law – thinks he did at twenty-three, and his son Anthony was born within a year of marriage, or in 1926, then Anthony would have been only fifteen when, as a young officer cadet, he was killed in the counter-attack on Tobruk' (Panthea Broughton, unpublished thesis).

As a 'solution' this commentator suggests that the evidence can be made to fit if we assume that Rickie was only twenty-one when he married. But this well-intentioned attempt is, I would suggest, quite beside the point. If Rickie had married at the – for a man of his class and education – unnaturally early age of twenty-one this fact would itself have been commented on, and in any case it still wouldn't make his son old enough to be killed in battle. Rosamond Lehmann has herself said that she did not keep any formal calendar of events in this novel; it is surely more realistic to conclude that mathematical accuracy is irrelevant and that the book is imbued with a subjective perception of time which owes something to the characters' feelings – the distancing effect of the war, cutting off the past – and something to the author's own standpoint. In 1946 it is not surprising that Madeleine and Dinah should feel that the events of even a few years back are remote and that those which belong to the pre-war period are part of another life. Such was the atmosphere of the late 1940s; as Dinah says at one point, 'the war and the bombing and all had ploughed up the past so thoroughly that nothing came back from it now but these – sort of stingless ghosts' (163). But it is also, I think, relevant that Rosamond Lehmann herself was writing the novel not in 1946 but circa 1951-2, when she herself was not forty-two like Madeleine but fifty. Her affair with Cecil Day Lewis, which was arguably the most important relationship of that kind she ever experienced, had ended two years earlier. One may be permitted to think that she was right – that, with the traumatic ending of that relationship and with the subsequent writing of *The Echoing Grove*, some cycle in her own life and work *had* come to a close, and that she lends this feeling, not entirely appropriately, to the younger Madeleine and Dinah.

No one who attempts to consider *The Echoing Grove* in the context of the writer's life can possibly ignore the significance of the relationship with Day Lewis; equally no one should make the vulgar and prevalent error of assuming that Day Lewis 'is' the faithless lover Jocelyn in the novel, much less that he is Rickie. It is true that originally Rosamond Lehmann was going to call the novel *Buried Day* (a title that survives in the French translation *Le Jour Enseveli*) and was only dissuaded from doing so at a late stage by the publisher, who pointed out that the public would place one interpretation only on this 'Freudian' slip. But, slips apart, *Buried Day* – like *Dusty Answer* a quotation from a Meredith sonnet – would have been a very good title for this book, with its preoccupation with time and its insistent imagery of buried things, both coming to the surface and interred for good. (The title that superseded it, *The Echoing Grove*, which is not a quotation but sounds like one, has been much munched-over by critics; it seems sufficient to say that it reflects – echoes? – Blakes's 'infernal grove' of love, and in general suggests the replications, repetitions and tricks of memory as in – to change the metaphor – a hall of mirrors.) What is fair, I think, to say is that, however much the betraying lovers Rickie and Jocelyn are based upon other experiences, older archetypes in the author's life, over all *The Echoing Grove* is imbued with a sense of triangular relationships which do find an undoubted parallel in Rosamond Lehmann's own life in the 1940s. Such situations were, in any case, a classic feature of the Second World War, when married couples tended to be separated, partially or totally, for years on end. Given that Day Lewis's wife Mary was then living in Devon with their two young sons while, unbeknown to her, her husband was living mainly with Rosamond Lehmann in London, one cannot help seeing a general parallel to Rickie Master's situation *vis-à-vis* his wife Madeleine.

[. . .] After Anthony's death, she could count on the fingers of one hand the times he had come to share the house with her [. . .] As the months went on he had seemed one might say to prefer to stay in London. He was glad enough to see her when she went up every ten days or so to lunch with him; but the only weekends he ever jotted down were those of Clarissa's half-term holidays . . . (166–7).

In September, Clarissa having gone to stay with a best friend, she went with Jocelyn to a farmhouse in the middle of Dartmoor. Fathoms deep in love, she scarcely gave a thought to her family. Rickie in any case had left London on another secret mission and was incommunicado. Very rarely during the remainder of the time left to him before his death did he return to the cottage. It was as if – she thought now suddenly, her heart turning over – he had been relinquishing his stake in it; by gradual stages, with no word said, vacating it (168).

But, as I say, the parallel is only general: it is Madeleine, not Rickie, who is then in love with someone else; Rickie and Dinah's passion has already wrought its destruction and is now spent. Among many other things, *The Echoing Grove* is an acute study of two people, locked together in an unsatisfactory marriage, who are emotionally and sexually on different cycles. Rickie has his all-consuming experience with Dinah in his late twenties and early thirties, while his wife is, in Georgie's subsequent words, '"just a married virgin . . . no, not that: she's a disappointed bride with three fine kids still wondering if this is all there is to sex"' (58). Later, while Madeleine is belatedly discovering the nature of sexual passion with Jocelyn, Rickie has entered what seems a prematurely middle-aged state of abstinence and passion spent. True, he spends a night with Georgie (the wife of an absent friend) three days before his sudden death in 1944, and makes love to her, but it is almost as if she is a stand-in for the long-estranged Dinah, and their night together and the conversation they have is not so much an event in its own right as a resolution and explanation of much that has gone before. Georgie, one might say, is Dinah on a different loop of time, and with a different face: she reminded Rickie of Dinah years before, when they first met at a party in a night club. The truth that, in life, we do not just experience people objectively as individuals but also as rôle-players in our own lives, returning again and again in different guises, is one that does not *quite* surface in *The*

Echoing Grove, but is permanently there in the novel, un-voiced, as it is in the totality of Rosamond Lehmann's work.

Repetitions – the echoes of *The Echoing Grove* – are ubiqui-tous in the novel: to speak of them, as some critics have, as if they were merely a matter of style or 'imagery' is quite inadequate; they structure the whole book, indicating by their presence the cyclic or recurring nature of events. Parallel situations abound: Rickie going to look for Dinah, Rickie going to look for Georgie; Rickie betraying Madeleine, Rickie betraying Dinah; Rob leaving Dinah, Jocelyn leaving Madel-eine; Mrs Burkett's feeling for Rickie, Rickie's feeling for his own mother; the way physical illness keeps intervening crucially in the course of events – Rickie thinks at one point: 'Strange how repeatedly the rhythm of this business had swung to physical disasters, the failure of the body' (142). When he collapses in Dinah's flat with a burst duodenal ulcer, and is thus prevented at the last moment from escaping into a new life with her, Dinah says to him: '"Your turn this time, darling"' (140), a reference to the fact that the previous time it was she who was carried off to a nursing home, after the stillbirth of Rickie's child, a failure which similarly and in more than one sense prevented the start of a 'new life'. (There had been a plan that Dinah, braver and more emancipated than her predecessor, Olivia, in *The Weather in the Streets*, should carry the child off abroad and bring it up there with a Bohemian friend, Rickie intermittently visiting this idyll.*) Madeleine and Dinah meet, as sworn enemies, over Rickie's bed in the nursing home, and do not meet again till, many years later, they achieve some kind of truce at their mother's death-bed. And Rickie's long, revelatory talk with Georgie three days before his death – a fate of which he himself seems

---

*It would indeed be possible to draw up a schema of parallel situations and recurring images *between* novels – a kind of master-plan of Lehmann-land.

to have some suppressed intimation – is paralleled by his own reminiscences then of 'a very silent uncle' (shades again of the Curtis family in the person of Uncle Oswald), who unexpectedly delivered himself of 'a perfect torrent' (223) of words and then died a few days later.

It is essential for the reader to accept that this is how the novel proceeds, not by chronological sequence, not even principally by a psychological time-scheme as in *The Weather in the Streets* (though elements of that are present as well) but, like a poem or a symphony, thematically, by repetitions, by patterns, by associative images. Readers and critics who have failed to understand this find *The Echoing Grove* disconcerting or diffuse, or merely 'depressing', or they complain at the 'complex' or 'confusing' way the story is told – not seeing apparently that the way in which the 'story' is told *is* the story, *is* the totality of the effect, and that with different telling the meaning would have been quite other and less. As Rosamond Lehmann herself has said, 'There is no such thing as an excellent badly-written novel . . . novels are made with words. With words we make the dragging net, the matter, the texture and the shape' ('The Future of the Novel', 1946). As Panthea Broughton puts it: 'It is the spacial form of this narrative which lifts events from melodrama and pathos and makes of them an intricately patterned work of art.' Yet such, apparently, is the hold that conventional, linear chronology has on the reading public, that even a sensitive and intelligent reviewer in *The Times Literary Supplement* could write when the novel came out:

The story itself is intricate enough, but it is further obscured by an approach that is consciously oblique. It starts near the end, and wanders backwards and forwards in time; important scenes are related in dialogue, at second or third hand; incidents are repeated, with a change of emphasis, revelations are withheld and motives gradually disclosed as in a carefully planned detective story. The problems posed by its complex structure and indirect exposition are answered with a variety of literary devices [. . .] (17 April 1955).

But the 'literary devices' *are* the structure. Nor is the basic chain of events particularly intricate, but in itself desolately simple. It is a useful exercise to examine the events chronologically – picking the story into its component parts – and then to see how, in practice, these events are presented to the reader.

Rickie Masters and Madeleine Burkett are born in the early 1900s and marry some time early in the 1920s – as already mentioned, exact dates should not be insisted upon. Fairly quickly, they have two little boys, Anthony and Colin. At this period, in the late 1920s, Madeleine's younger sister Dinah quite often stays with them and becomes briefly engaged to a suitable young man of their circle. ('"Oh the barrister, my fiancé!" She chuckled briefly. "What became of him? I'd forgotten his existence. Horrid man"' 284). Presently her clandestine affair with Rickie begins and

Dinah declared the engagement a mistake and without further explanation broke it off . . . she went to live on her own in a cheap room in Pimlico; wrote a subdued, not very interesting or well-written novel, semi-fantastic, about a deaf girl and a blind man, got it published;* enrolled herself as a student in some school of art: grew more and more cadaverous and uneven in her spirits; next went to live in Chelsea with a person called Corrigan – a woman as it turned out, a painter of only moderate talent and tendentious appearance, with whom she knocked around the pubs . . . And then, a thorough Bohemian, with a lot of impecunious, free-thinking-and-drinking, bright-witted, disreputables in tow, she started to come back into their lives . . . (16).

---

*Rosamond's younger sister, Beatrix the actress, who also, like Dinah, became a Communist, published a couple of now-forgotten novels in the 1930s. Rosamond Lehmann has told me that, when envisaging Dinah, she had Beatrix physically in mind, just as when envisaging Madeleine, she saw her elder sister Helen. But such identification should not be pushed too far.

Rickie became the rage and paid for all their drinks and bought at Dinah's prompting their ghastly daubs. [Madeleine's thought] [. . .] the truth was under my nose like a thing under a stone. I didn't lift the stone. It was forced up at last by what was breeding under it: the Thing, worm-generating, bedded in blood, roots, clay (181).

Dinah becomes pregnant, and the plan is made that she shall bear the child and bring it up with the help of Corrigan. But the baby is born early, in the middle of a snow storm through which Rickie struggles to reach Dinah, and it dies. Subsequently Corrigan betrays Dinah and Rickie in a letter to Madeleine: Rickie thinks:

Her large white powdered cheeks – obscene; her fine hard prominent brown eyes, her rubbery amplitudes of bust and hip bursting from grubby slacks and jumpers; her over-emphatic slang, her dirty stories, her roars of heartily yea-saying laughter, her romantic devotion to his cause and Dinah's, everything that revealed in her the *fausse bonne femme*, masked an aggressive Lesbianism. He might have known – he'd always known – she was a common fraud . . . (91).

We may seem a long way here from the Bohemian friends Olivia has in *The Weather in the Streets*, but it is essentially the same territory that is being viewed, with a colder eye.

Rickie confesses to his wife, but does not tell her about the dead child – indeed she never knows about it. None of the characters in this novel ever knows the whole of the story. He goes to see Dinah that evening; but returns to Madeleine, who receives him back. He is torn between the two women; Dinah is in a bad state, drinking heavily, and accosts him in the street. Rickie is sent abroad on business and there resolves to give up Dinah – who meanwhile takes to Rob, a young working-class drifter who has been befriended in her circle. While Rickie is away, Madeleine visits Dinah, and while she is there Rob seizes his opportunity to walk out. As always, there is something about Dinah on this occasions that makes her sister feel inferior or stupid, and she leaves without having had whatever show-down she was seeking. She spends the summer at her parents' house in the country; there she and Rickie, who comes for weekends, try to resume sexual relations, but it is not a success. Then Madeleine is called to South Africa where her father is seriously ill, and while she is there Rickie inevitably takes up with Dinah again – the Lehmann sick father opening the way, as before, for another relationship. Dinah has tried to commit suicide: she asks Rickie to take her away for a brief holiday by the sea to recover; he does so, and they fall deeply in love once more (see Chapter IX). When Madeleine returns, he tells her he wants to leave her for Dinah, a suggestion that is as ill-received as was Cecil Day Lewis's analogous proposal to his wife Mary in 1947. Rickie tries to leave, but the mental and physical stress of the whole situation catches up with him, and on his first night in Dinah's flat he has a haemorrhage from a duodenal ulcer. He is consigned to a nursing home, with the help of Dinah and Madeleine's mother, and after that his attempt to break up his marriage is tacitly abandoned. The sisters meet across his bed, but then do not see each other again for fifteen years. Rickie recovers, this time (to die after a similar haemorrhage in 1944). After his recovery, when he and Madeleine have patched up this relationship, Dinah makes one more call to Rickie: he goes to the flat he had rented for her in Bloomsbury, the flat where six months earlier he was taken ill, and there the relationship coolly ends. That evening Rickie and Madeleine attend a party with friends at a night-club, but Rickie leaves it abruptly to return to Dinah's flat, ostensibly to look for his cuff-links and probably to look for Dinah also; however she is not there. He returns home in the small hours, has a difficult conversation with Madeleine but finally gets into bed with her: as a result their youngest child, Clarissa, is born nine months later.

Meanwhile Dinah, abandoned finally by Rickie and deserted

again (the same day) by Rob, is visited by Selbig, a German-Jewish refugee living in the basement of the rooming-house in Stepney where she and Rob had lived – 'coming down silent with a reek of brandy to invade my free, my free-for-all body' (46). This awful day, with its initiation into 'the human condition, into freedom' (Selbig's concept), is the low point of Dinah's life, the apotheosis of her estrangement from everything that has made up the world of Madeleine and Rickie. It is from this spiritual death that she gradually, through the ensuing years, rebuilds some kind of structure for herself, marries a fellow left-winger, Jo Harman, of a different class and culture, is widowed, and acquires some kind of hard-won inner strength. Meanwhile Madeleine, living first in a rather semi-detached marriage with Rickie and then as a widow herself, brings up her children in the war-time country and discovers passion and love through a younger man, Jocelyn. It is after the war, on the very day, as it turns out, that Jocelyn is on the point of abandoning her, that Dinah visits her sister, and that is where the book begins.

So the book begins with the story's ending, in the section called 'Afternoon'. (The essential compression and circularity of the basic themes in this long drawn out human tale are indicated by the division of the novel into five sections named for the different times of one day, tenuously related to the November day in 1946 that Madeleine and Dinah spend in each other's company and also to the various times of day at which the key remembered events actually took place – one recalls the novel's original title.) In the first section the sisters gingerly pick up the threads of their long-broken relationship, leaving much unsaid. The viewpoint shifts between them, there are allusions to their mother, Mrs Burkett, the most fundamental link between then – whose death has provided the occasion for their re-meeting – and to their individual earlier and present lives; but we do not yet know what has happened. We infer, however, that it was to do with Madeleine's husband: ' "It's the piano – you remember it, Rickie's mother's wedding present." Now the name was said. Perfectly simple. Now the tension would begin to drop' (12). The sisters go for a walk, and Dinah's dog becomes involved in the churchyard in a battle with a rat – a patent if fluidly symbolic scene, over which a lot of portentous critical ink has been expended, although the general meaning is clear in the very words used, the comments and the action. The rat is finally disposed of, into the river. Dinah tells the dog

'Brave boy, you did your best. Your very, very best.'

'We all did,' said Madeleine. 'Our very, very best.'

They looked behind them at the now tenebrous graveyard spreading yet one more fold of everlasting night upon its shadow people. Dinah took a breath, as if to speak; said nothing; and Madeleine continued:

'The great thing was to get it out of her. I couldn't have done that. I admire you.'

'The great thing was to kill it. I couldn't. I'm sorry.'

We're sorry. We did our best. Stopped it going on dying; shovelled it into limbo. There's nothing more to be done, we'll go away. Darkness, close up this fissure; dust under roots and stones, consume our virulent contagion; silence, annul a mortal consternation. We must all recover.

But still the stones seemed rocked, the unsterile moulds, re-impregnated, exhaled dust's fever; a breath, impure, of earthbound anguish (29–30).

Clearly, what is being referred to here is not just a literal dead rat, but some enormous and agonising secret relationship/experience that has caused profound trouble to both women.

The next section, 'Morning', begins with Dinah awake in Madeleine's house in the early hours. She thinks of her niece, Clarissa, Rickie's daughter, never met, and then, by an extension of theme natural in this novel's construction, of another childbirth, that ended in death and burial:

'Let it alone, it's dead and everybody's dead except Madeleine and myself. It's a patch of scorched earth, black, scattered with incinerated bones. Whatever she's digging for will not turn up: there's nothing buried alive. What does she fear? . . . He fathered her breathing children in lawful wedlock and in the lawless dark another: mine . . .' (35).

This is the signal for us to move back in time and hear from Dinah's point of view about this birth. There is a brief reference to her period of trial, to later events, to Rob and Selbig, and then we move to 'That time when I summoned him [Rickie], the very last time' (38), and we see the bleak scene in the rented flat unfold, the keys given back and so forth. So, the very first time we see Dinah and Rickie together, they are estranged, and he is withdrawn and elusive, quintessential betraying male.

The same day then continues, from Rickie's point of view: he arrives home late, changes hastily and accompanies Madeleine to the pre-arranged night-club party with various of their married friends. (This is, incidentally, the evening when he first meets Georgie, the new American wife of an old Oxford friend.) The viewpoint shifts between Madeleine and Rickie, but there is the ever-present sense of the past and the future there also, both filling out the picture and subtly distancing the reader from it:

'How they laughed, what a sparking and crackle developed across that dinner table on that evening – Rickie the generator, the centripetal force. After his death, separated as they all were then by time and war, and too much preoccupied to miss and mourn him as long, as deeply as they would have wished, they did, each one of them, recall his mood that evening . . .' (56).

We get accumulated images of Rickie, the loving and the loved, through his friends' eyes: this is someone different from the man we have seen alone with Dinah. We also see Madeleine, through Georgie's eyes, as a sexually inadequate and frustrated creature, and then through the eyes of Tim, an old friend, as 'hot stuff all right – would be when she got into her stride' (69). They are both right in their own way, but only the reader will ever know that – it is by such juxtapositions that the book proceeds. We also see Rickie withdraw his sympathy from Madeleine while they are dancing and she says a sharp word to him; he walks out. In her good wife rôle Madeleine covers up for him. We stay with her viewpoint back in their London house; she goes to bed, he eventually returns. There is a painful scene between them, loaded with the echoes of other scenes that are yet to come (from our point of view) but Rickie explains his errand (the cuff-links) and manages to convey both his real anxiety for Dinah's well-being and the fact that their affair really is at an end: he and Madeleine make their peace; Clarissa is conceived. We move on to her birth, and this draws Rickie back in memory again: 'With a sense of shock he told himself that his last child had been stillborn: his by Dinah' (87). The earlier birth is then recapitulated from Rickie's point of view – the interminable drive through the snow to the West Country, till at last

through the bare succour of his finger-tips beneath her shoulder blades he was lifting her dying body into resurrection, he was all incandescent, ablaze with the pure total life of the world of death which to reach and save her he had traversed.

And that was the crack-up. He saved her through the power of love, and that was the end of the power of love. There was no way out for it, it had so overreached itself; it burst against negativity and was extinct (92).

Rickie is saved from his predicament of love, in a more mundane sense, shortly afterwards, when he is back home and is handed by Madeleine the betraying letter she has just received from Corrigan. The sequence of events then continues, as described above in chronological order, with

Rickie torn between the two women, making promises to both he is bound to break. He gets as far as discussing Dinah, and her drinking, with Madeleine, and notes to himself 'the similarity of the comments these girls made about one another' (115). Presently he escapes abroad and writes to Dinah telling her they must not meet any more, though all his thoughts are for her. He returns to England; presently there follows Madeleine's departure for South Africa and the resumption of his affair with Dinah. All this is told from Rickie's viewpoint, but when Madeleine returns and he nerves himself to tell her he intends to go away with Dinah we shift temporarily to Madeleine's viewpoint. Then back again to Rickie's as he goes to Dinah; there follows his physical collapse, bringing about as it does an ending to 'his stillborn freedom': 'He never saw Dinah again, he never heard from her or heard her name mentioned – until the day she summoned him to meet her at the flat' (142).

Having learnt all this, we then return to the rather later time, after Clarissa's birth, still with Rickie, as he lies in bed in the spare room. Now, the affair over, his thoughts go back to the very beginning, in that same room, in the days when Dinah was staying with them, and so that section ends.

When the next section, 'Nightfall', opens, we are with Dinah in 1946, again in a bed: 'And so all these years later, in another room in another house of his, vacated by him in perpetuity, lying awaiting no one in the bed [. . .]' The dead rat the dog caught earlier has been buried in the river. The next line runs: 'Rickie, thank God, was buried far from here' (145). Rickie's death, before only briefly alluded to, now begins to come into focus, with a passage seen from the viewpoint of Mrs Burkett, his mother-in-law. A conversation – about Dinah – between Mrs Burkett and Rickie is evoked, and then one after his death between Mrs Burkett and Dinah. Various critics of this novel have complained about this intermittent use of the viewpoint of characters that are dead by the time the story 'opens', a complaint which seems to me to misunderstand the fluid nature of perceived time in the book, and also the advanced and assured use of the shifted viewpoint. The cumbersome devices of Jamesian recitative in it are abandoned – but we do not return to the nineteenth-century omniscient authorial voice, but to a much more sophisticated use of varying consciousnesses.

We then move by a natural transition from Mrs Burkett to her other daughter, also waking in the night in 1946, and further details about her married past and the children, including the son Anthony's death, are filled in. We hear of Jocelyn; then of Mrs Burkett's recent death (another nursing home), and the re-meeting there with Dinah. From this, Madeleine's memory proceeds back again to the last time they have met: we hear about her visit in 1931 to the Stepney house to see Dinah when Rob was there. Speculation on the nature and point of Dinah's relationship with Rob carries Madeleine forward again to her own relationship with Jocelyn, then the image of Jocelyn carries her back again to Rickie on their honeymoon:

his face bent to hers, suddenly wild, dumb, brilliant against the whole Mediterranean sea and sky.
    'Rickie, what is it? Why do you look at me like that?'
    No answer (196).

With this, the section ends. The next, 'Midnight', is occupied entirely by Rickie's long meeting in 1944 with Georgie, partly from his point of view and partly from hers. Much more background is filled in, the nature of love is tentatively discussed and the concept of various characters – Rob, Selbig – forming 'links' in the story is broached, as if the bones of the whole book were now being exposed. We hear of a meeting that took place in the war between Rickie and Rob. Right at the end of this section, Rickie and Georgie's viewpoints are abandoned for what momentarily seems to be an authorial voice but turns out to be Madeleine's view once more, and we focus at last on Rickie's death. The contents of his wallet (from which, three days earlier, he handed Georgie the only incriminating scrap of paper) form a montage of the novel's themes:

[. . .] Some childhood snapshots of the boys – one including herself; a recent laughing one of Clarissa; two of his old home; also one he had never shown her of his mother as a pretty little girl with a fringe and a mane of fair hair, wearing a black yoked pinafore tied in at the waist and holding a kitten up to her cheek; also a letter: the good letter Jack Worthington [Georgie's husband] had written after Anthony was killed.

Touchingly trivial odds and ends to leave behind. All above-board, simple and clear as his blue English eye. Yet she had watched a stranger die . . . (268).

We are back with a variation of the image that concluded the previous section. Once again, Rickie had eluded her, and everyone else:

Last chance, last minute opportunity, chance of a life-time to resist . . . restore . . . Fight for him, fight . . . Call back. But stooping over him to speak his name, she found herself prevented [. . .]

His lids flew open. She looked into twin globes of crystal, shining without comment, without recognition; one moment lighting the finished portrait; then extinguished (269).

The final section, 'The Early Hours', takes place entirely in the present, though there are some reminiscences. It is overtly concerned with Madeleine's new problem with Jocelyn – which surfaces at that moment like a counterpart variant on the main theme in the last movement of a symphony. In more general terms, this section is concerned with the resolution and salvation of a friendship between the two sisters.

In keeping with the whole way in which this novel proceeds

is the use made of Rickie's cuff-links as both actual and symbolic objects. Like the rat in the first section, which has had to bear the weight of some over-dogmatic and eccentric critical interpretation, the links have been scrutinised so warily and exhaustively that some critics seem to have lost sight of the obvious fact that their function is after all to *link* one character with another, and one event with another. This is important in a story in which no single character knows of every event or indeed every other character: by the use of a linking object, passing like a talisman from one pair of hands to another, a pattern becomes clear in what otherwise might seem disparate and diffuse. We first see the jade cuff-links when Rickie has come to close the Bloomsbury flat and his relationship with Dinah in one and the same gesture. Dinah hands them to him, saying in pseudo-casualness: '"I found them in that drawer when I was turning out."' He appears to take them, but in fact leaves them lying on the arm of the chair and Dinah pockets them again, wordlessly: 'Already they looked incriminating – clues dropped, forgotten, in the room that saw the murder [. . .]' (41). Then, when Rickie gets home and is hastily changing for the night-club party, Madeleine mentions that she has not seen those links recently – but she is here not being suspicious, merely in her good wife rôle. At the other end of the evening, when he walks out on her while they are unenthusiastically dancing together, he goes back to the Bloomsbury flat, to return home between four and five in the morning to tell Madeleine: '"I went back to look for my cuff-links."' He has not, however, as he also tells Madeleine, been able to find them – or, by implication, Dinah either. Later in the book we learn that Dinah had taken them with her to the rooming-house in Stepney where she has been living with Rob and where, the same evening, she ends up in Selbig's brandy-reeking embrace. She has them clenched in her hand in her pocket; as he comes down upon her, '*I flung them*

over his descending shoulder, anywhere, let them go, anywhere,
I didn't hear them drop . . . I never looked for them' (298).
Much later, as Dinah tells Madeleine in the last pages of the
novel, when Selbig committed suicide just before the war one of
his last acts was to send the links back to her through the
post: Dinah had had no idea he had kept them. When she has
told Madeleine this, the two sisters agree they shall be passed
on to Colin, Rickie's surviving son – they had once belonged to
Rickie's father. To underline the symbolism of this, we know
by now that the design on the links is a Maltese cross, a sign
of forgiveness. And in telling Madeleine of Selbig's desire to
'save' her and of his lonely death, Dinah has also given a
further dimension to one of the book's central themes.

Rickie's death, the fleeting moment when we see 'the finished
portrait' before it is extinguished forever, is a key point in this
novel, which is death-haunted and full of images of stillbirth,
burial and resurrection. Dinah's perception, in 1946, that
'everyone's dead except Madeleine and myself', is almost
literally true. Not only is Rickie dead, and his firstborn Anthony, but so are Georgie, Rob – that 'stillborn soul', who
contrasts with Dinah's surviving soul – and Dinah's husband
Jo; so are Rickie's mother and Mrs Burkett; so even is Corrigan: 'Some pair of queens or other took her to Mexico and
she died there, years ago' (38). The birth which turns out to
be a death – Dinah giving birth to Rickie's child – is another
key point, and the words connected with life, death, inexorable
fate and the possibility of redemption cluster thickly round it.
Rickie has received Corrigan's coded telegram: 'Slight delay
now safe at destination come', warning him that all has not
gone according to plan, and as he sets out on his winter
journey the words dance and change themselves in his mind:

Severe delay: sudden delay: slight delay: serious delay . . . now safe,
not safe, now saved . . . which, which? Oh *destination*, ominous
word! *Come . . .* to the place she had reached, where it was appointed

that he should come to meet her. *I knew it all along*, he told himself.
I sent her to death, her destination . . . (91).

Dinah indeed attempts suicide a little later. But the truly
suicidal one, the one whose destination death is – and, in a
sense, the destination of the whole novel – is to be Rickie
himself: '. . . death running downstairs after him [. . .] Picked
up unconscious at the bottom, rushed to hospital, a burst
duodenal ulcer, too late, a few hours later he was dead' (43).
The point is fixed early in the book: the route by which he
reaches it, perennially tempting fate, failing to follow medical
advice, finally missing a crucial doctor's appointment, is indicated afterwards. Not 'what happens?' but 'how?'

The person we are shown most directly mourning for Rickie
is not Madeleine, nor Dinah, nor yet Georgie, but Mrs Burkett
his mother-in-law, who, in the tradition of Lehmann-mothers,
is in many ways very much a representative of convention,
decency and self-restraint:

'He was a good man. They are rare,' said Mrs Burkett; but emotion
choked her and she got up in a hurry and turned her back on Dinah;
who, lying stretched upon the sofa, had the tact not to ask her to
repeat herself, or delay her as she hurried from the room.
   Once safe in her bedroom, she addressed herself sternly, bathed
her eyes, blew her nose; then opened a locked drawer in her bureau
and took from it the vellum-bound book with gilt clasps in which at
intervals during her life from the age of eighteen onwards she had
copied out passages from her favourite authors. She read:

> Then look around
> And choose thy ground
> And take thy rest

took a pen and wrote under the quotation R.L.M., with the date of
his death; thus dedicating it to Rickie for his epitaph.
   It was not a broken life and not a failed one, she declared passionately to herself: he had chosen it with his eyes open and completed
it [. . .] (146).
   What they little realise, either of them, she told herself with a
vicious secretive spurt of triumph, is that Rickie knew that he and I

... that I understood him. No need to look facts in the face and call spades spades. We knew there was a link between us. Ah, why not acknowledge him – my spirit's son, as the twins, sons of my body, have never been? [...] (147).

In discussing this passage with me, Rosamond Lehmann has said that, yes, Mrs Burkett was meant to be 'a little bit in love with Rickie' and that, in contrast, Madeleine 'had a mother-in-law problem, and that is partly why Rickie has abandoned his heritage [and gone into the City] ... but I don't think I actually say so in the book. I should have.' She *does* in fact indicate it, but so late on in the account (281-2) that it comes rather too late for the reader to incorporate it into the overall picture. In general terms, however, the sense of interleaving family background and the thick palimpsest of different individuals' realities, each as valid as the other, is admirably conveyed. The fact that Mrs Burkett loves Rickie, in spite of what she knows or strongly suspects about his behaviour towards both her daughters, also strengthens the image of Rickie as the sort of person 'everyone loves', and this in itself is an important aspect of Rosamond Lehmann's declared view of novel writing. In her essay, 'The Future of the Novel', she remarked that whatever turns and changes the novel had undergone in the twentieth century, readers still wanted 'characters they can fall in love with'. And although her portrait of Rickie has been criticised as insufficiently rounded, I believe that, in this respect, she has succeeded admirably with him, not just by portraying him as 'charming' but by letting us see into his own heart, his own anguished capacity for love.

The *TLS* reviewer already quoted (17 April 1953) evidently felt Rickie to be insufficiently masculine, whatever is meant by that. In a long and otherwise mainly thoughtful review, he could not indeed resist poking fun at this hero to fall in love with:

Rickie's sex appeal has to be taken on trust, and his most apparent characteristic is an almost comical weakness and indecision in his love affairs [. . .] There is some talk of an office, and also a club, where his male life is presumably pursued; the only time when he is shown at his place of business is an occasion on which he faints. He plays in the story a strangely feminine role, almost that of a misunderstood and long-suffering heroine who inspires feelings of passion, chivalry and resentment in the more active sex [. . .] The searching examination of sex-relations is, for all its thoroughness, one-sided; only half the story has been told.

If this reviewer means that we are shown Rickie almost entirely in his husband and lover rôle to the exclusion of other aspects of his life, this is a fair criticism. When reminded of the gibe about the office Rosamond Lehmann smiled and said: 'Yes, it's true, I don't know anything about offices.' But if the reviewer is implying that Rickie's own attitude to sex and love is in itself insufficiently indicated, this seems to me nonsense. When the novel came out, Duff Cooper wrote to the author to tell her that she had succeeded, for him, in conveying 'just what men feel when they're in love', and this view has been endorsed by other men. The very indecisiveness, misnamed 'almost comical weakness and indecision' is in practice, many people would agree, an expression of a common and deeply rooted male dilemma. Men tend to be less strongly endowed by nature with the urge toward a close and monogamous relationship which is part of the female biological equipment for protecting home and children, yet their need for love can be just as great. In particular, a man of Rickie's class and type has been educated both for considerable freedom and autonomy *and* for considerable devotion to duty and all that goes under the heading 'honourable behaviour' (see Rollo Spencer as another example). The resultant conflict is not a personality defect but reflects what is finest in the man as much as what is bad. If Rickie is a victim, he is a victim of himself as much as of either Madeleine or Dinah. I cannot at all agree with the view of the novel expressed by (among other people) John Lehmann, when he wrote to his sister on its publication: 'the slaughter of all the male characters and the final comparing of notes by the two remorseless women who have tried to devour them doesn't entirely satisfy me [. . .]' This is surely in itself a one-sided view of what is in fact a much more general study of the capacity of individuals to mean well by each other and yet to inflict pain. Take, for instance, this passage near the beginning of the Georgie and Rickie section, which has the great and unusual merit, it seems to me, of conveying the almost absent-minded love-as-a-thing-apart nature of the male sexual drive as opposed to the centralisation of the female one – the very perception which some critics have suggested *The Echoing Grove* lacks:

[. . .] He could not say that he had remained chaste latterly from choice or out of principle. Every Government department including his own seemed to be stuffed with on-coming far from ill-favoured girls; he had taken several out to dinner, gone back to bed with one called Rachel: divorced, dark, hungry, clever, Jewish, rather beautiful; had had to retreat quite soon from an adventure for which he had only appetite not heart.

At the time – two years ago it must be now – when she had started to make it clear to him that she envisaged something tremendous, permanent, his basic emotion – underlying some affection, some gratitude, remorse, dismay – had been astonishment. How could she have imagined . . .? What could have so misled her? It was his need for love, she said, the way he asked for it. He was appalled. Of all the men she had ever known, she said, he was the most capable of a real relationship with a woman. If, as she guessed, he had been badly hurt, she could assure him he was not permanently damaged. Let him only surrender, be healed, not be afraid. He couldn't help feeling frightfully annoyed, he was not afraid – merely not prepared to harbour so much more than he had space or welcome for [. . .] (199–200).

It is, of course, indisputable that love – the 'chase', the 'war that brings nothing about' – is the central topic of the novel, as it is of all Rosamond Lehmann's novels. But that is not to say it is portrayed, in *The Echoing Grove*, in a parochial, woman's-angle manner. Love in this novel is love inexorably embedded in other realities, subject to destructive, alien pressures. Some readers, including John Lehmann, have regarded it as a saga of hopelessness, on which the final words can only be those lines from Blake that Rickie quotes to Georgie, which Dinah read to him and which he had once planned to have engraved for her on a bracelet:

> *And throughout all Eternity*
> *I forgive you, you forgive me.*

John Lehmann wrote: 'I wish I could feel that there was a tragic resolution or reconciliation as deeply felt as the suffering to balance it artistically.' Yet other critics – notably Panthea Broughton, whose work has already been cited – have traced in the novel, and particularly in the long Georgie and Rickie dialogue before death, a strong theme of salvation, even of a Christian frame of reference. Personally I have to admit that the evidence for this seems to me tenuous. Although the *words* associated with the Christian doctrine of Redemption are used – 'saved', 'annunciation', 'resurrection' – and there is indeed a persistent visual resurrection image as counterpoint to the images of burial, they seem to me to remain largely at the level of verbal echo and literary embellishment rather than anything more integral to the book's theme. Selbig, the central European refugee, 'with eyes like pits and hairy hands', who runs the rooming-house in Stepney, who gives Dinah phenobarbitone for a suicide attempt and whose idea of getting her to face the human condition is to force himself upon her, is not adequate as a mystic Messiah figure, even a failed one: '[. . .] He came to make me cry and make me drunk, and he did both . . . He wished to make me free of his rotting humourless world of wisdom and understanding, of pity for incurable humanity. Ach! Sometimes I think cynics do less harm [. . .]' (45–6). For all he is called in the same passage 'Saint, corrupt saint', he really does not seem much above the level of Corrigan. And in the passage near the end, already referred to, where Madeleine and Dinah are talking together and Madeleine says, 'Well, I shall not be saved', salvation, in spite of the resonances of the word, remains firmly anchored to earthly love. Madeleine is desperate not because of the human condition but because her lover has abruptly abandoned her. Half a page earlier, when Dinah uses the same term, it is a similar concrete context. '"Jo saved me," said Dinah. "Loving him – daring to love him. Being loved by him"' (286).

It is not to denigrate the undoubted general spiritual and personal benefits of this experience, to remark that, to achieve it, a co-operative Jo figure is necessary. Madeleine has indeed dared to love (Jocelyn) and her love has just been flung back in her face. It is a sad fact that, on the everyday, here-and-now, how-is-life-to-be-lived plane, Christian doctrines of Redemption through love are not particularly relevant.

Indeed, those who complain that *The Echoing Grove* is 'all about love' and is therefore (by implication) both unrealistic and humourless – like women at their traditional worst! – seem to be missing both the highly realistic descriptive element in the book and the ironic humour contained therein. Rosamond Lehmann always had a tough streak of this kind of perception in her, even at her most young and romantic – see the horribly convincing portrait of Mabel in *Dusty Answer* (quoted in Chapter III): and although this perception seemed to go into temporary abeyance in *The Ballad and the Source* it reasserts itself triumphantly in *The Echoing Grove*, and is indeed one of the many strengths of the book. There is a passage of blood-curdling honesty and bathos just after the 'saved' discussion between the sisters, in which Madeleine, glumly contemplating the rest of her life, fantasises two contrasted advertisements she might place in a magazine:

*Refined educated lady of good appearance (early forties) cheerful
disposition artistic tastes, widow (one child, girl, school holidays),
thoroughly domesticated, country lover, fond animals, experienced
cook gardener washerwoman, able drive car, undertake all household
duties, rough (coals, boots, wood-chopping, scrubbing etc.) not objected to ...'*
A perfect woman nobly planned.
*Emotionally frustrated unadaptable class-conscious matron victim
circumstances upbringing personal tragedies, exploited rejected
(grounds age, moral intellectual maladjustment) by lover renovating
sexual requirements, unwilling to accept suggestions re courage pride
eventual resignation, unable contemplate living a) alone b) for others
i.e. family friends community spiritual values or any other form
abhorrent vacuum, seeks instantaneous return status quo, failing
which immediate euthanasia ... (288).*

Alas, Madeleine in her distress seems to be dimly perceiving
a truth about the circular nature of traditional female existence
(as opposed to the extensible, linear, male model) loving,
bearing and rearing their children and then abdicating – or
being forced to abdicate by circumstances. The cycle which
this novel's whole form expresses is essentially a female cycle.
The 'cycle of experience' which Rosamond Lehmann felt had
opened for her in girlhood and was now, with the formidably
accomplished *The Echoing Grove*, coming to a close, is part
of Madeleine's perception also.

The range of characters in *The Echoing Grove* is wider than
in the other novels, and some of the most mordant verbal
descriptions derive from one character's view of another. A
sense of class and of different worlds alongside one another,
so present in Lehmann-land from the beginning, is here exploited to particularly good effect. Repeatedly, one character
is able to draw from another some response which has not been
elicited by those with shared cultural assumptions. Georgie,
originally a 'small town American girl', does this for Rickie;
Rob and Selbig, we must suppose, do it for Dinah. It is notable

that *all* the emotional relationships are in fact between people whose social backgrounds are not quite the same, and that frequently therefore their actions and reactions have a social meaning as well as an emotional one. In Rickie's case (as Dinah says) the difference between his background and that of his wife and sister-in-law is only slight, but it makes him upper-class rather than upper-middle-class (compare Rollo and Olivia) and turns him into something of a displaced figure without his Norfolk estate – sold to raise money, it is suggested, because Madeleine did not understand his attachment to it. Dinah, as part of her own cycle of collapse, disintegration and re-birth, becomes thoroughly *déclassée*, has an affair with the profoundly alien working-class criminal Rob, and then eventually is 're-born' into marriage with Jo Harman; but Jo himself is working-class and the whole world of East End Communism and Spanish Civil War-fighting that she inhabits with him is still part of her rejection of the values of both her own youth and Rickie's marriage. Here is Jo, seen through the eyes of Dinah's mother:

A dark plump glowing little man with intelligent eyes behind horn-rimmed glasses, a bright pink shirt, a loud check jacket and easy manners. Excellent teeth. Face expressive, mouth a shade too mobile. Hands cared for, sensitive. Warmth in his voice to compensate for the Jewish-Cockney twang [. . .] An affectionate boy, a good son, a taking little man. Interested in literature, in education: these they had discussed, not politics. What she remembered best were his shouts of laughter once she had got over the initial shock and put him at his ease. A laughing little man. 'Aren't you a duchess, though!' he said. His eyes teased, admired, delighted in her. 'I don't mind telling you I wasn't looking forward to this interview – though I'd made a vow I'd go through with it on my loney-own. I thought you'd be sure to come it over me, in spite of Diney saying no, not on the whole you wouldn't, not if I played my cards right . . .' (153).

All too soon he is to die, however, killed in Spain: 'Waste, tragic folly, criminal waste and folly' (154).

An element of social difference is significant in Jocelyn and

Madeleine's relationship. Rickie, who has never actually met Jocelyn, ruminates to Georgie on what his wife's lover may be like and how he may let her down – and it turns out that he is right:

'My guess is, he's a chap on the make. Quite a lot younger; humble background, scholarships all along. No harm in that. And bags of charm. But these ruthless, sharp-witted orphan types [. . .] It's not that they behave any worse than our sort – my sort – on the whole: it's just that they don't behave at all. Behaviour has ceased to be a concept. I've got a hunch they simply don't know what it feels like to feel *disgraced* – personal, moral, disgrace – dishonour if you like. You could say it was innocence, lack of humbug – end of the code of the Decent Fellow and high time too. Seems to *me* more like something left out, subtracted . . . like a dimension missing almost . . . She wouldn't know what to look out for, Madeleine wouldn't . . .' (228).

But though by that stage Dinah is worldly-wise enough to advise her sister, earlier we have seen her too adrift in a world alien to her own. It is significant that when Jocelyn has abruptly abandoned Madeleine for 'a grubby *New Statesman* girl' (see Chapter III), Dinah's brisk comment on his suggestion that he and Madeleine should go on meeting occasionally is '"How very common"' (291). Evidently, in spite of her vaunted Marxism, she has at heart retained the concepts of her upbringing. As she has earlier said to her mother: '"I couldn't be more thankful for the good sound upper middle-class stock I come of. It's meant a sort of solid ground floor of family security and class-confidence that's been a great standby"' (152) – an interesting, and no doubt true admission from a character who, for most of the book, has been presented as an outsider figure, a deliberate counterpoint to Madeleine's entrenched, sheltered wife-and-mother identity. Such is Dinah's appeal for Rickie, early in the novel we are shown him telling Madeleine so; it is indeed his first appearance:

Would he, she suddenly inquired, say Dinah was attractive? Yes he would – remarkably attractive [. . .] '*Really*, do you? . . . I suppose women can never tell about other women. She's not *pretty*, would you say? Or would you?' He was going to say it was her figure and she would answer yes, not bad if only she wouldn't go about so stiff and hunched; or her skin, and she would answer . . . But what he said, reflectively, was: 'She's mysterious.' 'Mysterious? What *do* you mean?' she drawled. He laughed as if to himself. 'She gives nothing away.' 'Oh I see. No, I suppose she doesn't.' She added judicially: 'What you really mean is she's secretive. Likes to cover her tracks. That's true. She always did. Cold natures are always secretive, don't you think?' To this he made no answer (15).

This scene has taken place far back in time, during Madeleine and Rickie's first year of marriage, when the affair with Dinah is still to come: it is evident that the rivalry between the sisters is something rooted in childhood, as if life had from the beginning cast them in opposing rôles. The suggestion that Madeleine, though conventionally good-looking, is gauche and sexually inadequate in a typically upper-class English way – the antithesis, indeed, of mysteriousness – is reinforced several times, and almost unbalances the telling of the joint tale in Dinah's favour. This is one of the endemic problems of the lack of an authorial voice: a perception of a person which may be distorted, in that it is the subjective view of one of the other characters, may nevertheless have sufficient force to impose itself on the reader as an ineradicable image. Here is Rickie's cold view of his wife when he had just come from his last encounter with Dinah:

Her head came round the door in a familiar gesture – peering on the threshold, goose-like, stretching her long neck as if to search out the lie of the land before advancing [. . .] Out of the corner of an eye he took in her appearance, thinking she looked a bit garish: petunia pink evening frock, a colour he disliked, white fur wrap, diamond clips and earrings, make-up over done, blue-shadowed eyelids between frowning forehead and hard anxious stare. She was beginning to plaster it on, he thought, like all the rest of them. All but one. One pale one. White moth among Painted Ladies, quite out of place in this our life . . . (46).

Who can win against a unique, pale moth, particularly one who – it eventually transpires – has embarked on a successful sex life at an early age in a way unusual for girls of that class at that period? Yet it is Dinah we see 'behaving badly', taking to drink, being in fact ditched by not one lover but two (Rob as well as Rickie, and on the same day). Essentially, it seems to me, the clue to Madeleine and Dinah, superficially so different, is that in origin they are not separate people at all: they are two aspects of their creator's own personality, Lehmann-woman divided up, so to speak, into her component parts, her successes and defeats rearranged in a new and meaningful pattern. It is significant that Rickie, who, of all people, might be expected to see them in quite different lights, ultimately lumps them together: '"I . . . wronged one of those girls rather more than the other"' (259). And significant also that, near the end, the division between the sisters seems minimal, their separate experiences at last forming one synthesis.

Yet, although Madeleine might technically be said to have come out of the whole business with more credit and less loss, it is Dinah who sticks in our minds as the one holding the trump card: she is the one with 'mystery', she it is who is, in the words of another man to another Lehmann-woman (Gil to Rebecca in *The Ballad and the Source*) 'so nice and dark'. She it is who has at least dared to explore strange regions, socially as well as in the heart: '". . . Listen," I would have said, "I'm in trouble, I'm not up to anything; I'm frightened. I'm in the hands of crooks, thieves, perverts, *murderers*. I've been living in dreadful lodgings . . ."' (39). It is to her, in fact, that Rosamond Lehmann has assigned her own essential 'outsider' properties, for the outsider is also the adventurer and this Madeleine will never be. Dinah tries to *create* something for herself – a life, a world, a personality – and by the end of the novel has succeeded, not triumphantly but adequately. Madeleine's only aim has been to acquire a ready-made position for herself and hang on to it: '"I was always afraid to look . . . I don't know what at. At myself, I suppose. Or sex – particularly sex. But seeing I was considered so very pretty, I blindly hoped I might get by. Or rather it was a double thing: I *assumed* I would; but all the time I was convinced I wouldn't . . ."' (283). It is the difference between the woman with energies and ambitions beyond her specifically female needs, and the woman whose entire concentration is upon these needs. To Dinah are given the more obviously 'feminine' qualities of sexuality, yet it is Madeleine who, for all her prickliness, is a wholly female and therefore wholly vulnerable character – more so than any other Lehmann-woman.

We have met the outsider before in Rosamond Lehmann's work, in many forms. There is one passage in *The Echoing Grove* which, apparently unimportant in itself, seems to me to suggest a chain of links going back to one of the author's earliest images – a for-all-time child outsider figure in which all the adult ones, such as Olivia, such as Dinah, have their origin. It is Mrs Burkett (that benign mother-figure, embodiment of long-term insight) who produces this:

For the first time, and with a pang whose edge bewildered her, it struck her that she could trace a family likeness in Dinah after all: to her little sister Alice, fifth among the brood of nine – plain child (quaint was the word used then), the only sallow one; when she was six they cut her hair short because it grew in rats' tails; once tamed a hedgehog for a pet; loved newts and toads; once dug a tunnel under asparagus bed hoping to reach Australia, got into trouble; always in trouble; once after disobedience punished by governess, ran away from home, was brought back mud-and-rain-drenched after dark by postman; died in her tenth year of meningitis ... What trick of feature, facial angle or proportion, accidental pose, expression, could have summoned back that long-forgotten child (159)?

Apart from including also the dead child motif so central to Rosamond Lehmann's imagery, whom or what does this vignette recall? Obviously Cherry, in *The Ballad and the Source*, that wayward child who leaves oddments in matchboxes around the garden, who is an 'outsider' in the sense that she is not like her prosaic brother and sister and may have had a different father, and who dies of meningitis at a similar age. But, beyond Cherry, I would suggest that the quintessential concept that is being summoned up once again is that represented by Chrissie Wyatt (see Chapter 1), that passionate, infantile embodiment of some principle beyond the ordinary: seeking, wanting, clutching, telling stories, inventing symbols, dreaming dreams.

When writing of Chrissie I have remarked that, though her family have really identifiable originals in the author's childhood, she herself does not – that Chrissie, the heart and point of 'The Gipsy's Baby' is a creation from some other realm of the writer's fertile mind. Readers who have followed me this far may themselves, by now, have some idea themselves where Chrissie comes from. It is she, after all, who is the permanent outsider, the forerunner of all those other more disguised outsiders that haunt Rosamond Lehmann's work, the outsider that lurks like an uncomfortable ghost in the heart of Lehmann-woman, even when she is apparently at her most happy and successful. Even love, her paramount obsession and need, cannot rescue her entirely from the influence of this ghost, for it is an ineradicable part of herself – the part that makes her a writer. It is the element in Rosamond Lehmann which is responsible for the very existence of the novels, and yet it is the element which, within the artistic compass of those novels, has to be concealed, dissembled, pushed aside: such is the central paradox of the writer's life experience. It is indeed the writer who is the permanent outsider.

In conclusion

In pursuit of Rosamond Lehmann's themes – the pattern on the carpet – I have perhaps neglected to make some simple points about her novels that a reviewer newly come to them would feel it important to state. If I have failed to say how readable her books are, how vivid and how true to life many of her incidental descriptions, and how purely funny and enjoyable – even richly humorous – are many of her passages, that is not because I regard such things as unimportant. It is rather that I take for granted that her work has this instant reader appeal in addition to its other, more profoundly analysable aspects. I also take for granted that most of those who are likely to read these pages will have been brought to do so by the very fact that they already know her work and appreciate its attractive qualities. For those who do not, I hope I have quoted often enough and liberally enough to give some impression of the treat in store.

Nor do I mean the phrase 'instant reader appeal' to sound dismissive. A novel is a marketable artefact and must work as such, whatever its other, more long-term functions. Indeed, a degree of readability might be regarded as a *sine qua non*: no matter how cleverly and subtly a book is constructed, it will not find its audience – will not achieve its basic function of communication – if it is just too hard, too boring, too unattractive or impenetrable to its potential readership. (Most readers will be able to supply their own personal list of writers who, in their view, fail to some extent in fulfilling their basic aim and, by definition, one who fails significantly is unlikely to be published anyway!) It is true that a good novel is written essentially out of an inner compulsion, an urge to create a particular mental picture, to deliver a message (albeit oblique or equivocal) about the nature of life. Indeed novels which are *not* born of such compulsions and imperatives, however 'readable', 'well constructed' or 'amusing' and so forth they may be, never really succeed, even in their own terms, because the most vital part of the construction is missing. Nevertheless the fact remains that every novel exists not just in its own right, as the product of an individual consciousness, but also as the product of a particular society, period and set of ideas about the nature of fiction. Novels are produced to be published, read and *enjoyed* (whatever the spectrum of emotions contained within that elastic word). They are not just transcriptions of life, though they are frequently discussed as if they were – by critics both perceptive and obtuse. They are indeed artefacts, and paradoxically the more unforced and true-to-life a novel may seem ('Oh Miss Lehmann – that's my story exactly!'), the more art, skill and discipline are likely to have gone into its making.

This is true not only at the level of plot-construction and the evolution of theme – an area in which the choice of what to omit is as important as the choice of what to include. It is also true at the level of words and phrases. I have already quoted Rosamond Lehmann as saying: 'There is no such thing as an excellent badly-written novel . . . novels are made with words. With words we make the dragging net, the matter, the texture and the shape' ('The Future of the Novel'). The unusual but apt image of the 'dragging net' creates for us a concept both of selection and of trawling within the writer's own experience: this image is in itself an example of what Rosamond Lehmann is saying – she has chosen the words carefully. In conversation, she has remarked to me that, to her, 'every word is important'. Her method, in producing her novels, has been to write several drafts, each one a 'pared down' version of the previous one, saying the same thing in a richer, more concentrated form. The evolution of her style has been an instinctual and yet a stringent process, a matter of 'listening . . . to the rhythm and beat of each sentence.' Readers (and there have been quite a few of them) who have imagined that her novels have somehow gushed spontaneously from her personal experience without the transforming and refining pressures of art, have been very much fooled – though one should add, I suppose, that such a fooling, the art that conceals art, is in itself part of the novelist's business.

The novels have sold well – though none as spectacularly as the first, *Dusty Answer*, which so caught the feeling of the times. Both it and *The Echoing Grove* are published now by Penguin: the two books represent different poles of her achievement but (as she herself remarked) are to some extent complementary. *The Echoing Grove*, indeed, has been in Penguin for a good many years, and its presence on academic reading lists has been one of the ways in which Rosamond Lehmann has surfaced again into public visibility. The other novels are all now currently available as Virago reprints. Of these, *Invitation to the Waltz* and *The Weather in the Streets* have sold the best, as they no doubt deserve to.

Rosamond Lehmann's literary revival is still underway, and although she is in some respects a survivor from another era, enjoying the unusual experience of basking in a renown that seems posthumous in character if not in fact, it is still too early to make any pronouncement on the niche she will eventually occupy in the English Literature of the twentieth century. In addition, the fact that she *is* still alive, and still intensely interested in life and literature, inevitably makes my task one to which no proper 'Conclusion' can be written. The 'finished portrait' (to employ the phrase she employed in her valedictory passage on Rickie Masters in *The Echoing Grove*) comes only with extinction. (Not that 'extinct' is the word she would now use, but it is the one used in that context.) The corpus of her work is as it is: it is unlikely now that much will be added to it. But it is not impossible – and in any case a writer's books, considered as a function of her life, are not in themselves entirely 'finished portraits' but are to some extent still volatile. It may yet be that further developments in Rosamond's own life, or aspects of that life which can only be adequately revealed and discussed after her death or the deaths of others, will shed further and different light on her novels. Till that time, the present book should be looked on as something in the nature of an interim report – and one which has had the peculiar advantage of having been read by the subject herself.

Meantime, she has contributed something in the nature of an interim report herself, in her memoir *The Swan in the Evening*, which is sub-titled 'Fragments of an Inner life'. I have quoted a number of passages from this book, mainly in order to support and amplify my thesis about the interrelation between her life and work: I have not till now considered the memoir as a shaped and constructed artefact in its own right. It may be objected that a memoir is an attempt to tell 'the truth' whereas a novel is 'fiction'. Yes, but fiction is simply another way of putting truths down on paper, and *The Swan in the Evening*, in selection of themes and construction, is certainly as carefully and deliberately shaped as any novel.

Its overt theme is Rosamond's own childhood (Part I); the mechanisms of fiction; the childhood of her daughter Sally (together in a brief, fugitive Part II); and an exposition of her belief (Part III) in Sally's continuing existence. This major concept is expanded in a fourth part – an open letter to her grand-daughter Anna, Sally's niece – and, in the Virago edition that was reissued in 1982, in an Epilogue correcting one or two points and bringing the theme up to date.

The sub-text of the memoir is, I would suggest, the idea of death itself, and the pattern by which the awareness of death surfaced in her life from early childhood. If life is a writer's material, then death must inevitably be the ultimate tough subject, the Last Thing which each writer confronts – or avoids – in his or her own way.

Among other things, *The Swan in the Evening*, a non-novel which yet shares many of the salient characteristics of the author's novels and is intimately related to them, is itself a victory over a disintegration which it documents. In Part III, when writing of the 'well-nigh total seize-up in such powers of self-expression as I have', which Sally's sudden death provoked, Rosamond wrote cogently as if her very grief were an unwritten – and unwritable – novel: '. . . inquiries for my "next book", however solicitously meant and gratefully acknowledged, could only act as one more turn of the screw. At times I had the actual physical sensation of a solid book-like object bound in stiff boards with cutting edges and sharp corners stuck in my midriff. Sweat, groan as I might, I was stuck with it for ever.' (89)

Like, indeed, a child dead in the womb, that recurrent and prophetic image from her novels. What Rosamond Lehmann did eventually bring to birth, in 1967, nine years after Sally's death, was not therefore a novel but this memoir, constructed like a novel from 'surreptitious scribblings – memoranda, notes, recollected images and sayings . . . an underground hoard . . .' And since the central event of the memoir is Sally's death, the patterns formed by this are perceived as running backwards in time as well as forward: the theme is not just the way in which this life-altering event has affected her subsequent thinking, but the way in which the pattern was in some sense 'there' from the beginning. Her own childhood, as she describes it, though rich in pleasures and even idyllic moments, is also haunted by intimations of mortality: the dead bird, the coachman's dead daughter, the death too of a favourite shop-assistant who is murdered by her True Love:

'in the field where the old brick-kilns stand he cut her throat'. (Two Lehmann-themes coming together with a vengeance there, in the lover who murders love and life itself.) In addition, there is a well documented generalised fear of dark, aloneness, non-being, and a horror of separation from loved ones so intense that when her mother and elder sister were due to go on a trip to the United States without Rosamond no one dared tell her till the very moment of departure had come.

At the opening of Part II (a section which evokes Sally's own sudden childhood fear of death and separation) Rosamond writes:

What I have put down so far might almost be called sub-autobiographical. It has been like a descent into a vault or cave or crypt, where all is darkness when you first penetrate. Then a torch flares, light is thrown here on a painted fresco, there on a carving or bas-relief: figures in a landscape, real and recognised, yet each with the mystifying impact of a symbol-in-itself, pure of interpretation and interpreter; and able to be caught only just on the outward side of verbal or pictorial existence. Any attempt to treat the findings, or to expose them to more air and light might cause them to vanish altogether (65).

Such indeed is the cavern of memory and experience from which creative works are essentially drawn. But in the event, and in consequence of Sally's death, Rosamond Lehmann *did* come to treat the findings, and expose them to the relative air and light of an organised and heartfelt belief-system. And whatever the meaning and importance of this in terms of her own life, such a step is essentially inimical to the novelist's endemic quest for truth, the manipulation of metaphor and symbol, the covert questioning and uncertainty that drives the creative writer onwards. Regarding her belief in life after death, Rosamond herself admits, in the memoir which is ultimately a celebration of this: 'I . . . might well have felt that I owed it to my integrity to remain sitting on the fence.' Well, yes. But of course one does not really have any choice in these matters.

To me, Rosamond wrote, after reading the bulk of this present book:

I don't know – but I must say that, to me as a person, *The Swan in the Evening* is totally relevant, in that my entire life as the 'outsider' of your book ceases with the experience of Sally's death and after. My obsessions with dead babies, children who will die, abortion etc . . . obsessions you point out with the most embarrassing correctness, all fell out of my psyche, or were re-interpreted. Underneath all these obsessions lay my lifelong obsessive search for the meaning (if any) of life and death. I didn't *hope* or *fear* any more, or dramatize the subject. Like Jung, I didn't – I don't – believe: I know. So I've become a sort of insider – a strange sort.

It seems fitting to leave the last word thus with her.